The King of Prayers

A Commentary on The Noble King of Prayers of
Excellent Conduct

SHAMAR RINPOCHE

Series

Bird
of
Paradise
Press

ABOUT BIRD OF PARADISE PRESS

Bird of Paradise Press is a non-profit book publisher based in the United States. The press specializes in Buddhist meditation and philosophy, as well as other topics from Buddhist perspectives including history, ethics, and governance. Its books are distributed worldwide and available in multiple languages. The bird mentioned in the company's name is said to be from a special place where beings can meet with favorable conditions to progress on their path to awakening.

Also by Shamar Rinpoche

BRINGING MIND TRAINING TO LIFE
An Exploration of the 5th Shamarpa's Concise Lojong Manual

THE PATH TO AWAKENING
How Buddhism's Seven Points of Mind Training Can Lead You to a Life of Enlightenment and Happiness

BOUNDLESS AWAKENING
The Heart of Buddhist Meditation

BOUNDLESS WISDOM
A Mahāmudrā Practice Manual

A GOLDEN SWAN IN TURBULENT WATERS
The Life and Times of the Tenth Karmapa Choying Dorje

THE KING OF PRAYERS
A Commentary on the Noble King of Prayers of Excellent Conduct

CREATING A TRANSPARENT DEMOCRACY
A New Model

BUDDHA NATURE
Our Potential for Wisdom, Compassion, and Happiness

A PATH OF PRACTICE
The Bodhi Path Program

The King of Prayers

A Commentary on The Noble King of Prayers
of Excellent Conduct

SHAMAR RINPOCHE

*Edited by Julia Stenzel, Thea Howard,
and Lara Braitstein*

*Prayer translated under the guidance
of Shamar Rinpoche
by Pamela Gayle White*

RABSEL
PUBLICATIONS

Contents

Preface

In December 2009, on the occasion of the Kagyu
Mönlam Chenmo in Bodh Gayā, Künzig Shamar
Rinpoche gave a teaching on the *Sangchö Mönlam*, the
Noble King of Prayers of Excellent Conduct, also known
as the *Samantabhadra Wishing Prayer*. In Sanskrit it
is called *Ārya Bhadracaryāpraṇidhānarāja*, in Tibetan
phags pa bzang po spyod pa'i smon lam gyi rgyal po.
It is the final part of the *Gaṇḍavyūhasūtra* which is
itself the last section of the *Avataṃsakasūtra*. Buddha
Śākyamuni gave the teaching of the *Samantabhadra
Wishing Prayer* to urge practitioners to treat the
great Bodhisattva Samantabhadra as a role model to
emulate so that all their wishes may be accomplished.

—*Publisher's Note*—

This text includes a number of Sanskrit terms with diacritical marks. A brief pronunciation guide appears here.

Long vowels (ā, ī, ū, ṝ, ḹ) are pronounced for an extended time with some emphasis, for example, "dharma<u>kāy</u>a."

ṛ and ḷ act as vowels, such that they can appear between two consonants, and are pronounced more or less as they would be in English, with ṛ resembling "ir" or "ri."

ṅa is pronounced as a nasal "nga." **ña** is pronounced as "nya."

ca is pronounced as "ch" in chair. The consonant **cha** is pronounced as a softer "ch" sound with more aspiration.

Retroflex consonants (ṭa, ṭha, ḍa, ḍha, ṇa) are pronounced as their English equivalents, but with the tongue curled back towards the roof of the mouth.

Aspirated consonants (tha, pha, and so forth**)** are pronounced by adding a puff of air to the initial sound.

śa is pronounced as "sh." **ṣa** is pronounced as "sh" with the tongue curled back towards the roof of the mouth.

ṃ appears at the end of a syllable and produces varied sounds: "m," as well as other nasal sounds that vary according to the following consonant. For example *saṃgha* is pronounced "sangha."

ḥ acts like a brief echo found at the end of a syllable, adding a "h" sound followed by the preceding vowel, for example, muniḥ is pronounced "munihi."

Throughout this book, Sanskrit and Tibetan terms appear in italics when attention to their meaning or spelling is needed, or when they appear as the titles of texts. Words that have broader usage in the English language, as well as proper names of people and places, appear in regular typeface with diacritical marks.

Where Śāntideva's *Bodhicaryāvatāra* is quoted in the commentary, our editors have cited Pamela Gayle White's translated excerpt on page 4, and the Padmakara Translation Group's edition (*The Way of the Bodhisattva*, Boston: Shambhala, 1997), adapted on page 19, and quoted on page 50. The verses for each section are noted in the text.

Two terms appear in this commentary which are not defined within the text: *Bardo* is a Tibetan language term referring to an intermediate state, in this case the intermediate state between death and rebirth. The ten *bhūmis*, literally grounds, are the ten stages of a bodhisattva in progress to enlightenment. These terms are explained in many sūtras, with a clear, concise presentation in the *Jewel Ornament of Liberation* by Gampopa.

Introduction to the Prayer

THE SIX PARAMITAS

The practice of the six *pāramitās*, or the six perfections, is the heart of the Mahāyāna path. Even if we practice only one of the pāramitās in a proper way, it will include all the other pāramitās. If we practice, for example, the pāramitā of generosity, we will donate possessions and resources. If we give with pure motivation, we are practicing ethical conduct. If we give alms without tiring, without feeling hardship, we are practicing the pāramitā of patience. If we give every day, as a long-term practice, this is an example of practicing the pāramitā of perseverance. If we are not distracted while we practice generosity, we are practicing the pāramitā of meditative concentration. If we give without attachment to the *three spheres*, that is, the recipient, the donor (ourselves), and the object given, we are practicing the pāramitā of wisdom. Thus, in one single act of generosity, each of the six pāramitās can be accomplished.

The practice of the pāramitās can also be subdivided into ten pāramitās. In this system we break down the pāramitā of wisdom more finely into four separate components. These are aspiration, skillful means, power, and timeless wisdom. The *Noble King of Prayers of Excellent Conduct* is the heart of the pāramitā of aspiration and thereby a component of the pāramitā of wisdom. By practicing it we can tap into the power of the wish-fulfilling accomplishments of great bodhisattvas, such as Samantabhadra, who have already mastered the pāramitās and who are therefore able to bestow the blessings of their accomplishments. Just as the correct practice of generosity includes all the other pāramitās, the practice of the pāramitā of aspiration also includes them all.

DISPELLING THE THREE OBSTACLES

In this practice of the pāramitā of aspiration, it is very important to understand that the timeless essence of our mind is pure and unstained by karmic obscurations. This timeless essence of mind already contains all the qualities we need for attaining ultimate enlightenment. It is like a mirror. If all the dust has been removed from the mirror, the true reflection of the mind will stand out very clearly.

In our normal samsaric state, our mind is clouded by ignorance, which causes clinging to the illusion of a truly existing self. Due to this ignorance, many emotions— what we call *kleśa* or mental afflictions— arise, and these lead to accumulating various wholesome and unwholesome actions. Since we don't understand our mind, we become attached to the objects grasped, as well as to the mind which grasps. As we act, we plant imprints in our mental continuum. When the time is right, these will come to full maturation. Fully-matured karma is the principal reason for us to travel in cyclic existence, or *saṃsāra*. In other words, our mind's contamination has three different aspects: the first one is the contamination of kleśa; the second one is the contamination of latent karmic imprints in our mind; and the third aspect is the consequences, that is, the fully ripened results that we have to experience. These three aspects of mental contamination are responsible for our continuing uninterruptedly in saṃsāra. Metaphorically speaking, these three obstacles are like the dust on the mirror that prevents the true reflection from coming through. We need to practice diligently to eliminate them.

How do we overcome and remove these three major obstacles? The best antidote is the pāramitā of aspiration. The pāramitā of aspiration is a balanced combination of wisdom and skillful means, which is a very rare and effective tool for practice. However, we must understand that we need a few preconditions before we can actually accomplish this pāramitā. The first very important precondition is the bodhisattva vow.

THE TWO PRECONDITIONS

Bodhisattva Vow

—the first precondition—

There are two different kinds of bodhisattva vows: The first is the aspiration bodhisattva vow; the second is the application bodhisattva vow. When we take the bodhisattva vow, we try to emulate all the bodhisattvas' great wishes. Taking the application bodhisattva vow means, we follow in the footsteps of all the buddhas. Just as they did, we practice bodhicitta, aspirations, and the pāramitās, in order to realize the same accomplishments that they have realized. When we observe both bodhisattva vows in a pure way, then, even in our deep sleep, our merit and wisdom accumulation will continue to increase spontaneously, giving rise to conditions necessary for our pāramitā of aspiration practice.

How do we take the two kinds of bodhisattva vows of aspiration and application? There are two different transmission lineages that were handed down by Buddha Śākyamuni. The first one passes from Buddha Śākyamuni to Maitreya, the future Buddha: According to this lineage, the aspiration and application bodhisattva vows are transmitted separately in two different rituals. In the second lineage, which was transmitted via the great Bodhisattva Mañjuśrī to Lord Nāgārjuna, the two aspects of the vow are transmitted in one instant. The verses for transmitting and receiving this particular bodhisattva vow are extracted from the great master Śāntideva's work *Bodhicaryāvatāra*, or *The Way of the Bodhisattva.* By reciting these particular verses three times, you receive the bodhisattva vow of Nāgārjuna's transmission. We recite:

> *Until I reach the heart of enlightenment, I take refuge in the Buddhas. Likewise, I take refuge in the Dharma and the assembly of Bodhisattvas.*

> *Just as the Buddhas of the past developed enlightened mind and progressively trained as bodhisattvas, I too will develop enlightened mind, and train progressively in order to help beings.* [2.26 & 3.23-24]

Prior to receiving the bodhisattva vow, we must first obtain the refuge vow. In the Mahāyāna tradition, we take the refuge vow with these words:

> *Until I reach the heart of enlightenment, I take refuge in the Buddha, as well as the Dharma and Saṃgha.*

The common way of taking refuge is a promise for our present lifetime. We promise to take refuge in the Buddha, Dharma, and Saṃgha as long as we live. The bodhisattva vow, however, extends from now until we reach ultimate enlightenment. Thus, when we take the refuge vow in combination with the bodhisattva vow, then the refuge vow also applies from that very instant until the attainment of ultimate enlightenment.

—*Bodh Gayā*—

The holy place of Bodh Gayā is the place of enlightenment of the perfect Buddha Śākyamuni, the Blessed One, the Bhagavān. He was born as Prince Siddhārtha, the son of King Śuddhodana.

He lived in the city of Kapilavastu in great luxury, but, being completely detached from all the wealth and prosperity of his royal family, he gave up his lifestyle and pursued the practice of the six pāramitās, superior meditative stability, and superior wisdom. During six years on the banks of the river Nairañjanā he practiced austerities, after which he achieved the vajra meditative absorption, which is the level of ultimate enlightenment of buddhahood. Pilgrims who come to the bodhi tree, the tree of his enlightenment, receive the excellent blessing of the place of Buddha's awakening.

Therefore, when we have an opportunity to go on pilgrimage and we visit a holy place like Bodh Gayā, we should contemplate the Buddha's accomplishments and enlightenment, and view him as a role model that we should follow. We do not idolize the Buddha like children idolize their parents—we are not worshiping an idol—nor do we treat him in a superstitious way as a god who will bring us to a happier place, but we contemplate all his vast accomplishments and what he underwent, and we follow in his footsteps as we sit here today listening to the teachings. To follow the Buddha's example, the aspirations of Bodhisattva Samantabhadra are indispensable. Studying them, however, doesn't mean we are able to actualize them. To that purpose, we need to have taken the excellent two-fold bodhisattva vow and to practice the perfections that lead beyond this world to perfect enlightenment.

NON-APPREHENSION OF THE THREE SPHERES

—the second precondition—

The second prerequisite we need to know is the particularly sublime method called "the non-apprehension of the three spheres." We must realize the illusory nature, or absence of self in all phenomena. This realization takes place at three different levels, called the "three spheres." In brief, this three-fold understanding means that ultimately there is no self, no sentient beings whom we are trying to benefit, and no relationship that exists between the two. For example, when we give something to others, or when we make aspiration prayers, we need to understand that the beings we are praying for, as well as we ourselves who are praying, and the words we recite, have no essential reality and therefore we must free ourselves from any clinging or attachment to any of them.

It is very hard for beginners to even imagine this. Therefore, we have to start with the practice of meditative absorption. Once we become skilled in meditation, we will begin to get an understanding of the absence of the "three spheres." Without meditation, all sentient beings, down to the smallest insect, have the natural impulse to cling to an idea of self. The root cause of all clinging to a self is ignorance. If we analyze what we take for a self, we also realize that it is without definable substance. We find our idea to be vague and confused— the self is illusory. When we analyze whether the assumption "I exist" is true or not, we discover that we are taking as real an idea that has no basis at all. It is only our confused mind that grasps at this concept as real. That is why the person who is praying has to understand that there is no object that can be grasped as "I, me." There is nobody who can be referred to when we say or think "I am," or "I know." Likewise, other sentient beings also mistakenly cling to an "I" and are bewildered. One should not hold the thought that they are "other." In the prayer, we wish to manifest in the form that is appropriate to benefit others, and we wish that all other sentient beings who are in saṃsāra may be benefited through our prayers.

Our prayers can bring benefit to others because of dependent origination. Other than that, the words of the prayer and their meaning also do not have an intrinsic reality. It is part of our practice to contemplate dependent origination, and thereby understand that things have no essential reality. Thus, we pacify our clinging to them. There is no better method to undo our grasping. When we are without grasping and attachment, our prayer becomes the practice of the perfections that will take us beyond saṃsāra. The meaning of *pāramitā* is to go beyond saṃsāra, that is, attaining the first bodhisattva level and onward; the prayer is the cause for this attainment.

Even if we say the prayer with grasping and attachment, we accumulate merit, but we cannot accumulate wisdom. Having perfected the accumulation of merit, we will attain higher rebirths in saṃsāra, but we will not be able to attain liberation from cyclic existence. In order to attain true liberation from saṃsāra, one needs to accomplish the cause *beyond the world*, which is the previously explained realization of the three spheres. The correct understanding of emptiness applies to all sentient beings, to our ego-clinging, and to the relationship between the two. Thus, if we are motivated by the understanding of the illusory, essence-less, insubstantial nature of beings, then we will be free from greed and attachment when we practice the six pāramitās and the pāramitā of aspiration. Being free from greed and attachment, we will correctly practice the accumulation of merit and wisdom, which in turn will lead to the wisdom that will definitely liberate us from saṃsāra.

Explanation of the Prayer

Structure of the Prayer

The *Noble King of Prayers of Excellent Conduct*, also translated as *Samantabhadra's Wishing Prayer*, was taught by the perfect Buddha Śākyamuni. When the translators, the Tibetan *lotsawa*, translated this prayer into Tibetan, they first paid homage to the great Bodhisattva Mañjuśrī, asking for assistance to translate the prayer successfully.

The entire aspiration prayer contains three sections: (1) the preparation, (2) the main body, and (3) the conclusion. The first part, the preparation, consists of the seven branches, which are an excellent means to accumulate the roots of virtue and the cause for bringing about the fruit of the aspirations. Just as we need to first plant the seeds and then have conducive weather in order to have a successful harvest, likewise we need the seven-branch offering prayer in order to reap a successful harvest of accomplishments.

The second part, the main body, elucidates all the aspirations made by the Bodhisattva Samantabhadra. The third part, the conclusion, is the dedication.

Overcoming Ignorance

It is important to understand our inborn ignorance and the role it plays in our taking birth in saṃsāra. As explained previously, it is because of ignorance that we are unable to realize the true nature of our mind. We create our own idea of a real self, and we cling to it. Based on this erroneous idea, we take both external phenomena and the internal grasping mind to be reality. External phenomena are sensory perceptions such as images, sounds, odors, tastes, and touch-sensations. These external phenomena are not real, but are merely reflections in our mind. Via the six sensory faculties, namely the eye, ear, nose, tongue, body, and the mind faculty, we gather mental data in the respective six consciousnesses. The seventh consciousness, which is called the "obscuration consciousness," has the function of communicating all the impressions gained within the six sense consciousnesses into the basic consciousness, or *ālaya-vijñāna*, and it is during this process that it deludes each and every impression with the idea of self-existence.

The obscuration consciousness is therefore the most subtle and deep-rooted mental affliction in our mind; it continually maintains a mistaken belief in a self, and it is the basis for all coarse emotions and the feeling of self-importance. The eighth consciousness, called "ālaya-vijñāna," is the ground of all, and it is the holder of all the seeds, whereas the other consciousnesses are its projections. Due to our mental defilements and karma, we collect an unimaginable variety of latent, habitual tendencies; these are the imprints or seeds in our basic ālaya consciousness. When these come to maturation they give rise to their corresponding confused impressions of the three samsaric worlds: the world of desire, the form realm, and the formless realms.

This process is comparable to a dream: the deepest impressions of the day are those which express themselves in a dream. The weak latencies will find only weak forms of expression. Likewise, the strongest impressions among the mental defilements, and the karmic impressions accumulated under their influence, are planted in the ālaya consciousness. When they come gradually to maturation, the fully ripened physical body takes its confused existence in samsāra.

If we look at samsāra and its various realms, we see that they are inundated with many different kinds of suffering. For example, in the animal realm, due to the ripening of previous negative karma, beings are endowed with an animal body. They are trapped within an animal body, and experience all kinds of suffering due to this particular form. Upon death, although they depart from their animal body, their consciousness still persists and carries on in future rebirths. Whatever is the strongest karmic consequence in the ālaya consciousness will dictate what the next rebirth will be. Because of our belief in the idea of a self, mental defilements and emotions leave strong imprints in the ālaya consciousness, and it is then very difficult for beings to attain a positive rebirth in future lifetimes. A fortunate rebirth is the direct result of the accumulation of good karma.

So how do we free ourselves of the vicious cycle of rebirths, and, in particular, of rebirth in the lower realms and their endless suffering? How do we overcome this problem of creating contaminated imprints in our ālaya consciousness? The only way is to break away from dualistic perception. Our mistaken and habitual dualistic mode of perception defines our confused mind, and gives rise to the negative thoughts and emotions that bring about our suffering. Generating bodhicitta for all sentient beings is the only way to overcome this subtle but persistent obstacle. The numerous enlightened masters who have come before us taught countless methods on how to go about this. All these various methods and skillful means are summed up in the seven-branch prayer. This prayer, or rather practice, offers us a succinct summary of how to overcome and subdue the mental defilements, and how to accumulate the merit that will finally free us from the suffering of being trapped in a samsaric existence.

The *Noble King of Prayers of Excellent Conduct* can be analyzed and explained in an extensive manner. However, for a simple and sincere practice, such details are not needed. It is sufficient to contemplate the power of the aspiration of Bodhisattva Samantabhadra from the verses of this prayer. If we follow the example of Samantabhadra in his wish fulfillment and aspiration power, we can overcome the confused states of the bardo and accomplish the five different levels of learning and practice, and ultimately the ten bhūmis of the bodhisattva's practice. Therefore, this is one of the most direct and effective methods.

THE PRAYER—PREPARATION: EXPLANATION OF THE SEVEN BRANCHES

The First Branch:

Paying Homage

In all of the worlds in all ten directions
Reside the tathāgatas of past, present and future.
Before each and every one of these lions among men,
I bow down joyfully with body, speech, and mind.

We start by paying homage, not only to Buddha Śākyamuni, but to all the tathāgatas in all the worlds and in all the ten directions. They are referred to as "lions among men." This metaphor expresses the idea that the lion reigns supreme among all the animals. Just so, the buddhas are unrivaled, and reign supreme in the entire human realm.

The phrase "all ten directions" expresses the limitless nature of the dwelling places of the buddhas. There is not a single pure realm that is not part of the ten directions. All those pure realms are the result of the buddhas' wishes to benefit beings in a completely spontaneous and perfect way. The pure realms are the natural, effortless fulfillment of the buddhas' activities, but can be perceived only by highly developed spiritual beings. Beings with too little merit, who are born into this world and experience suffering, can rely on the Buddha who has come to this world, has taught the Dharma, and whose teachings have persisted until today. These beings are born with a human body and have the conditions and capacities to follow the teachings. Although the pure realms can only be accessed by those with great purity in their minds, through gradual purification of their defilements and karma, all sentient beings are potentially able to experience these pure realms.

When we practice this first verse of the prayer, we visualize the limitless pure realms of all the ten directions, where the buddhas of the three times—past, present, and future—reside. As purely as possible, with our body, speech, and mind, we pay homage to all the buddhas of the pure lands.

By the power of wishes of excellent conduct,
Each buddha evoked becomes manifest.
With as many bodies as atoms in the universe,
I bow down deeply to the victorious ones.

It is important to remember that whatever positive activities we do, such as prostrating and paying homage in front of the buddhas of the three times, past, present, and future, we should do so with a genuine pure motivation, as well as with firm belief and faith. We visualize that all buddhas are in the space in front of us while we make prostrations.

We also visualize ourselves manifesting in as many bodies as there are atoms in the universe as we perform the prostrations together with all sentient beings, touching the ground with our forehead, hands, and knees in front of the buddhas of the three times.

Atop one particle, as many buddhas as particles
Are settled amidst bodhisattvas, their spiritual heirs.
Thus dharmadhātu, the entire sphere of being,
Abounds with the buddhas that I have envisioned.

How do we use the mind to pay homage to the buddhas? Doing this visualization is a particular practice method; it is a powerful tool for the accumulation of merit and wisdom.

—Discussion of the Dharmadhātu—

Dharmadhātu literally means the realm of phenomena, or the expanse of reality. It is the dimension of reality that lies beyond dualistic perception, the same as suchness, or emptiness.

For ordinary beings, phenomena appear in a definite size and number. Material objects, moreover, appear as solid; they have definite colors, and seem to be independent objects outside of our mind. However, if we examine our preconceptions, we realize that whatever we perceive can be nothing else but an image in our mind. Solidity, colors, shapes, and so on, are merely mental phenomena. Nobody ever had a direct perception of solidity. And since phenomena are not as they appear to us ordinary beings, we call our ordinary, unenlightened experience of the world "mistaken dualistic manifestation." Once we accept that "our world" is merely a mental experience, notions of big and small do not apply anymore, and our mind can hold any number of these manifestations. It is this capacity of our mind to extend itself beyond any limit that we have to use for our practice. In this way, we are approaching the truth of the dharmadhātu.

For instance, in a small and confined room, we can imagine a large city. In one short minute of a dream we can develop a very complicated, elaborate story, which, if we wanted to write it down once we woke up, would require a lot of paper. If our ideas of size reflected truly existent reality, how could we experience a large city in a small room?

However, if we understand that our mode of conceptualization is erroneous, then we can free ourselves of its trap. We can transform our minds to be very effective tools for the accumulation of merit and wisdom by going beyond our ordinary concepts of size and quantity. In our practice, we will simulate the reality of the dharmadhātu by visualizing the universe in its infinity of minute particles. Modern scientists have shown us that the entire external universe can be broken down into atoms and molecules. On each and every one of these atoms, we envision a countless number of pure lands, where the buddhas reside together with an entourage of bodhisattvas, arhats, pratyekabuddhas, and disciples. Then, with sincere dedication, we prostrate with our body, speech, and mind to all these limitless buddhas and bodhisattvas in all the countless pure realms.

We should not get intimidated, doubting whether we are capable of developing such a visualization—we are doing it already all the time. It is like the example of a large city appearing in the dream of a person who is confined to a small room. In our aspiration practice we should tune into the dharmadhātu, so to speak, pushing the limits of our experience and envisioning the infinity of space as pure lands.

Using every tone of a multitude of melodies
I revere them with boundless oceans of acclaim.
Singing the praises of those gone to bliss,
I honor your qualities, O victorious ones.

After paying homage with our body, we do so with our speech. We continue to visualize the dharmadhātu filled with countless pure realms, where buddhas reside with their entourages of arhats, bodhisattvas, pratyekabuddhas, and others; and with the most melodious of speech we praise all the enlightened merits and accomplishments, which are by nature beyond measure. Just as limitless ref lections can appear in a mirror, without the mirror appearing congested, so all the buddhas and their entourages also can dwell in limitless pure realms on countless atoms without appearing crowded. We venerate these buddhas with boundless oceans of praise.

In the *Noble King of Prayers of Excellent Conduct* we use the term "ocean" many times. "Ocean" does not refer to the Pacific Ocean, but was used as a term of measurement in ancient India, referring to an inconceivable number. Water is comprised of atoms, and the metaphor of the ocean expresses the unfathomable number of atoms that make up an ocean. And when singing our praises in various melodies, we offer the best possible sound; a sound like that of Sarasvatī's vīṇa. Her musical instrument produces the most perfect and melodious sound in the world.

The Second Branch:

Praising and Making Offerings

The second of the seven branches comprises two aspects: praising and offering. Regarding the offerings, there are two kinds: material offerings and the unsurpassable offering of Dharma. With the following verse we make material offerings.

Sumptuous flowers, beautiful garlands,
Precious parasols, fine cymbals and balms,
Radiant lamps and the most fragrant incense:
I offer them to you, O victorious ones.

In the first line the Tibetan word *dam pa* occurs twice. It means "good" and "genuine," and here it is translated as "sumptuous" and "beautiful." The word *dam pa* implies that when we offer, our offerings should not be contaminated by attachment, greed, or regret over having made these offerings. Moreover, we do not offer objects that were stolen or acquired in any other improper way. The objects we offer—f lowers, garlands, beautiful parasols, beautiful instruments like cymbals, fragrant incense, and so on—represent the most precious objects and substances that we consume or use in our lives. The importance of offering all these to the buddhas is not that the buddhas require or demand them, but rather that we need to practice non-attachment towards these objects. We offer in order to purify the attachment to our possessions.

Such wonderful arrays, all perfectly presented—
Exquisite apparel and sweet-smelling perfume,
Jars of scented powder piled high like a mountain—
I offer them to you, O victorious ones.

We offer "exquisite apparel," which has the ability to cool a person when it is very hot outside, and to keep one cozy-warm when the weather is very cold. We offer "sweet-smelling perfume" and wonderfully "scented powder." These refer to the best quality sandalwood perfume, and the most precious combination of floral scents. We also offer the most delicious food, all being "piled high like a mountain," like Mount Meru. We present all these on the very best offering plates and cups, such as we would use to give offerings to a king.

These vast and superlative offerings
Express my confidence in all of the buddhas.
With the strength of conviction in excellent conduct,
I bow and present them to the victorious ones.

This verse refers to the unsurpassable Dharma offering. Material offerings can be offered by normal sentient beings like us. However, the unsurpassable offering of Dharma can only be made by the bodhisattvas on the ten bhūmis because of their vast accumulation of merit and wisdom, which gives them the power of aspiration. Being the continuation of wishes made by past and present Buddhas, these are aspirations to benefit all sentient beings, who are as countless as the atoms of the universe. The supremacy of the gift of Dharma was expressed by the great master Śāntideva in his *Bodhicaryāvatāra* with these words:

If the mere intention to be of benefit to others
Exceeds in worth the veneration of the buddhas,
Then what need is there to mention actual deeds
That bring about welfare and happiness of all beings
without exception? [1.27]

Accomplished bodhisattvas are able to work in manifold ways for others. For example, they can manifest a wish-fulfilling tree that will grant all the positive wishes of sentient beings. Such activity is the result of their vast power of aspiration, derived from their meditation practice, and can only be done by bodhisattvas. For normal practitioners along the path, there are three ways in which we can generate unsurpassable offerings. The first one is to generate bodhicitta. The second is to commit ourselves to learning and understanding the Buddhadharma. The third is to carry out Dharma practice and master it. By making these three kinds of unsurpassable offerings, common practitioners on the bodhisattva path are able to gather a vast accumulation of merit and wisdom in the form of ultimate offerings.

The Third Branch:

Repentance

Whatever misdeeds I may have committed
Through body and speech, as well as through mind,
All outcomes of passion and anger and ignorance:
I openly disclose each and every one.

Repentance is a powerful antidote for overcoming our weaknesses, correcting our mistakes, and purifying whatever negative karma we have accumulated since time immemorial, throughout our countless lifetimes. All of us ordinary sentient beings prefer to see only our positive sides. We don't want to see our mistakes or face the negative aspects of our character. Because of pride and self-consciousness, we remain blind to the true problem. When we confess and repent our unwholesome deeds, we first of all face our weaknesses and mistakes, which then enables us to improve, and finally to overcome them. During the confession, as explained previously, we imagine ourselves, as well as all the buddhas in the pure realms, as countless as the atoms in the whole dharmadhātu. We then acknowledge and vow to disclose all the negativities that we have accumulated through pride and selfishness.

The Fourth Branch:

Rejoicing in the Merits of Others

I rejoice in each occurrence of merit produced
By buddhas and bodhisattvas of all ten directions,
By pratyekabuddhas, by those training on the path,
By arhats beyond training, and by every single being.

Rejoicing in the merits of others is one of the most powerful tools of merit accumulation. It doesn't come naturally, because our pride and clinging to a self usually keeps us from recognizing other people's merits and accomplishments. In this practice of rejoicing, we recognize and take delight in the qualities of other beings, and also in the merits of all the accomplished practitioners, such arhats and buddhas who have mastered the five levels of practice and have attained the arhat level. We also rejoice in the pratyekabuddhas, who have practiced the Buddhadharma for a hundred kalpas, and helped to spread the Dharma in a land that is without the presence of a buddha. We rejoice in the greatness of the bodhisattvas, who collected vast accumulations of merit and wisdom for three eons before they attained enlightenment; and we rejoice, of course, in the merits and accomplishments of the buddhas who manifest the three *kāyas*, or bodies of the Buddha.

The Fifth Branch:

Requesting the Buddhas to Turn the Wheel of Dharma

O lanterns who illumine worlds in all ten directions,
By way of the progressive stages of awakening
You have become buddhas, free from attachment.
Protectors, I entreat you all: turn the supreme wheel.

By requesting the buddhas to turn the wheel of Dharma, we are wishing for beings to be able to attain the *nirmāṇakāya* level. We recollect the dharmadhātu as consisting of limitless particles on which, in pure realms, limitless buddhas and their entourages reside. We also multiply ourselves while praying, and we request the buddhas to turn the wheel of the Dharma, in the same way as Buddha Śākyamuni descended into our human realm and turned the wheel of Dharma for us.

The Sixth Branch:

Requesting the Buddhas to Remain

Palms joined, I beseech those among you
Who mean to manifest the state beyond suffering:
For as many eons as there are atoms in the universe,
Remain for the welfare and happiness of all beings.

While reciting this verse we continue to manifest ourselves in as many bodies as there are atoms in the universe. We make a very humble but dedicated request for buddhas not to pass on to nirvana but to continue to benefit all sentient beings. Through this very powerful aspiration and request, sentient beings will be able to attain the *saṃbhogakāya* pure land, with all the five different merits that are attached to that pure land. Again, this is a very powerful aspiration tool.

The Seventh Branch:

Dedication

Whatever small merit has been garnered here
Through prostrating, offering and disclosing,
Rejoicing, entreating and beseeching,
I dedicate it all for the sake of enlightenment.

The dedication is one of the most important aspects of Buddhist practice, and therefore also of this prayer. The dedication of merit is a vehicle that enables practitioners to attain all the three kāyas of the Buddha: the *dharmakāya*, the *saṃbhogakāya*, and the *nirmāṇakāya*. When we offer all the merit and wisdom accumulated in the previous six branches, we again visualize ourselves as limitless as the atoms of the universe, and we offer the merit towards the enlightenment of all sentient beings equally.

The saṃbhogakāya and the nirmāṇakāya forms are the buddhas' spontaneous manifestations for the benefit of sentient beings, similar to the sun coming out and giving light to the earth in a spontaneous way without effort. Their activity is the fruit of their accomplishments throughout the different bhūmis of the bodhisattva path. It is the power derived from their accumulation of merit and wisdom over three eons. As Milarepa said in one of his songs: When you are a yogi practicing in the mountain cave and you dedicate the merit of your practice to your sponsor who lives as a lay practitioner of the Buddhadharma in a city, when you finally reach enlightenment the result for both of you will be essentially the same because of that dedication. Therefore, we should dedicate all the merit accumulated equally to all sentient beings, following the example of Milarepa. According to Śāntideva in the *Bodhicaryāvatāra*, dedication is the same as making wishes. We wish that all beings may attain a healthy body, freedom from sickness and obstacles, freedom from suffering, and that all their positive wishes may be fulfilled. The power to fulfill such wishes is derived from the vast accumulation of merit.

The dedication becomes perfect through the generation of bodhicitta and through realizing the emptiness of the one who dedicates, the emptiness of others, and the emptiness of the act of dedication, that is, the previously explained three spheres. This is the ultimate method of the dedication branch.

THE PRAYER—MAIN BODY

Main Aspirations of Samantabhadra

The main text of the prayer starts with the verse:

May the buddhas of the past and those dwelling presently
In the worlds of the ten directions be honored by offerings.
May those yet to come swiftly fulfill their aspiration
And attain buddhahood through the stages of awakening.

During the practice of the *Noble King of Prayers of Excellent Conduct*, we should generate a pure mind and genuine motivation. Moreover, throughout the whole prayer, we should continue to visualize the dharmadhātu filled with countless atoms on which buddhas reside in their pure realms, complete with their entourages of arhats, bodhisattvas, and other disciples.

In the first verse of the main body of the prayer, we wish that all present and future accomplished practitioners—whether they are in an accomplished stage (the first to the seventh bhūmi), or in the stage beyond training (the eighth, ninth, or tenth bhūmi)—may quickly accumulate all the merit and wisdom necessary to attain total enlightenment. By the power of our previous offering and dedication, and through the strength of our sincerity, we wish that they swiftly attain complete buddhahood.

Wherever there are world systems in the ten directions
May they, in their great number, become perfectly pure.

The world systems in the ten directions refer to the previously explained dharmadhātu, which is filled with atoms that accommodate the pure lands of buddhas, with their entourages of bodhisattvas and accomplished practitioners. These countless buddha realms within each atom do not appear crowded at all. Just as a drop of water contains a multitude of beams of sunlight, and just as in our dream a brief thought can encompass a vast array of events, we visualize that the contaminated world of saṃsāra is, through our pure wish and practice, transformed into the Buddha's pure land. We do have that mental ability to transform the world.

Milarepa once performed a miracle in front of Rechungpa. He manifested his entire body in the horn of a yak. As he was meditating in the horn of the yak, the horn did not become any bigger, nor did the body of Milarepa become any smaller. Nevertheless, this did not pose a problem for the manifestation. It was possible because the concept of big versus small as being polar opposites of each other, this dualistic mode of perception, is just a concept derived from our delusion. If we can go beyond this ignorance—as we have been trying to do through the practice of the seven-branch prayer by visualizing all the buddha fields contained within each and every atom—then transformation is possible. Dualistic perception is mistaken and illusory, derived from our ignorance. Visualizing the buddha realms in every minute atom is a vast accumulation of merit. If we can visualize only *one* buddha realm, the merit is already great, not to mention visualizing all the buddha realms in the ten directions. Planting such imprints in our ālaya consciousness can effectively eliminate our ignorant clinging to a self, and thus pave the way for our liberation from saṃsāra and ultimate enlightenment.

**May these universes abound in victorious ones
Who have come before the tree of enlightenment,
Accompanied by bodhisattvas, their spiritual heirs.**

In these lines we contemplate the accomplishments of all the past buddhas. We make a very strong and pure wish that all future buddhas may follow in the footsteps of the past buddhas, in that they will become enlightened under the bodhi tree and turn the wheel of the Dharma for all the disciples.

May each and every one of the manifold beings
Of the ten directions always be happy and healthy.
May all beings find true purpose in the Dharma,
And in harmony with this, may their hopes be fulfilled.

This wish addresses all sentient beings in the ten directions. We wish that they may attain a precious human rebirth and have the chance to come in contact with Buddhadharma: that they may come face to face with a Buddha, learn about the Dharma, and practice not only for their own benefit, but also for that of all sentient beings.

May I carry out the many forms of enlightened conduct,
And remember past lives when experiencing each new one.

When we generate bodhicitta, both aspiration and application, we accumulate vast merit. Due to the power derived from this, we will attain a precious human rebirth in all our future life times and we will remember very vividly our wishes and experiences of our past lives. An example illustrates this power of recollection: a few centuries after the Buddha's time there was a great master, Vasubandhu, who was the abbot of Nālandā Monastic University. He taught continuously and in the window of the class room sat a pigeon, who always listened to Vasubandhu's teachings. It took great joy in this. After that pigeon passed away, it attained rebirth in human form, as a child living near Nālandā University. The first few words the child spoke were, "My teacher is Vasubandhu." This is one of many experiences that show how generating bodhicitta and learning Dharma enable us to remember experiences of past lives.

During each successive death, transmigration, and rebirth, May I always embrace religious life, and renounce.

This verse refers to practitioners who have generated bodhicitta, and who have made a wish to renounce saṃsāra and worldly life in order to help others. Without an attitude of renunciation, which is a result of little desire and self-grasping, how could we be able to be of genuine benefit to others? Buddha Śākyamuni, the greatest renunciant, led the life of a *bhikṣu*, a fully ordained monk, and has taught this path to his followers as a safe path to liberation and an ideal condition to serve sentient beings in all life times.

Following the example of the victorious ones, May I fully accomplish excellent conduct, And may my moral behavior be flawless and pure. May I conduct myself faultlessly in all situations.

The Buddha possesses a special retinue of his closest bodhisattvas, called the eight great bodhisattvas. Besides Samantabhadra, there are Mañjuśrī, Avalokiteśvara, Vajrapani, Maitreya, Kśitigarbha, Ākāśagarbha, and Sarvanivaranaviśkambhin. They all are worthy of being emulated. In the *Ākāśagarbha Sūtra*, or *Namkha'i Nyingpo Do* in Tibetan, the pure conduct of a Mahāyāna practitioner is explained in great detail by the Buddha. We should study this sūtra in order to learn what it means to follow in the footsteps of the great bodhisattvas.

Whether a practitioner is a disciple or an accomplished master, they emulate the role models of past buddhas and bodhisattvas and follow in their footsteps by generating the two kinds of bodhicitta, aspiration and application, and the path of the ten pāramitās taught by them. In this verse, we particularly make the wish to have flawless and pure moral behavior. Ethical conduct is a requirement so that we never lose our bodhicitta. Bodhicitta will guide us along the path of the ten pāramitās until we will be able to genuinely benefit all sentient beings.

May I communicate the Buddhadharma
In every language known to sentient beings,
The tongues of gods, nāgas, djinns, trolls,
And all languages spoken by humankind.

With this stanza we pray to use our capacity of communication to benefit all sentient beings. The practice of the pāramitā of generosity consists of three kinds of generosity. The first is giving away our wealth and possessions. The second is fearlessness, which means helping others to overcome obstacles and protect beings from fear. These two kinds of generosity can only remove temporary obstacles. They do not solve the root cause of sentient beings' suffering. Only the third kind of generosity, the giving of Dharma, can solve the root problem and enable them to reach ultimate enlightenment.

The exceptional capacity of communication referred to in this stanza is attained on the first bhūmi. Bodhisattvas who have attained the first bhūmi can in one single instant manifest one hundred pure lands, and in one hundred buddha forms, they teach the Dharma in various languages, such as the speech of *nāgas*, djinns, trolls, and all languages spoken by human beings.

Gentle and wise, may I apply myself
To the transcendent qualities of the pāramitās,
While never losing sight of awakening mind.

Although we are just humble disciples, we make a pure and strong wish that in all our future rebirths, we will never lose our bodhicitta which is the very basis and foundation for attaining complete enlightenment. We develop the bodhisattva's attitude to benefit all sentient beings by generating perseverance and wisdom, and rejoicing as we practice and learn about Dharma. We are so moved by the Dharma teachings that we have tears in our eyes or spontaneously weep when we listen to the instructions. This bodhicitta generates positive karma and is the basis for attaining ultimate enlightenment. We make the wish to progress, using these various skillful means, and to attain the different bhūmis.

As for all harmful acts that have resulted in veils,
May they be entirely purified, without exception.

In addition to never losing sight of, and continuously generating bodhicitta, we need to be mindful in order to eliminate all the obstacles, which are the results of our negative karma that we have accumulated since beginningless time. The worst obstacles result from the so-called "four black deeds." The first of these is cheating one's guru, or the Three Jewels—the Buddha, Dharma, and Saṃgha. The second black deed is harming or distracting another practitioner's bodhicitta practice. The third black deed is slandering one's guru or another bodhisattva. The fourth is instigating a conspiracy to break up the harmony of the Saṃgha. These are the extremely evil deeds that result in prolific negative karma and tremendous obstacles.

May I be liberated from negative karma,
Disturbing emotions, and the actions of māras.

Negative karma will derail our progress along the bodhisattva's path. It will harm whatever positive merit we have accumulated and cause obstacles along the practice path. Most of the time, the confused mind does not know how to effectively counter mental afflictions such as greed, ignorance, aggression, and so forth. We allow them to take over our mind and cause us to do innumerable negative deeds, big and small, thus creating endless negative karma. With this verse we make a very strong wish that we be protected, and ultimately free, from all these. The bodhicitta we have generated is very precious. We pray that our bodhicitta be guarded carefully, and that it is not contaminated or harmed by any of the kleśa.

Wherever there are world systems and beings,
May I be like the lotus, not clung to by water,
And the sun and the moon, unhindered in the sky.

The lotus flower is used as a metaphor to illustrate the bodhisattva's conduct along the path. Bodhisattvas are not far removed from sentient beings. They don't all live in mountain caves, but are very close to all beings and always have the desire to help and to liberate them. Lotuses have their roots in dirty mud, but yet, their pure white blossoms remain pristine and untouched by the mud. In the same way, bodhisattva practitioners along the path are not contaminated by the habitual tendencies and karma of the sentient beings they are trying to liberate.

If we harbor no hatred, no anger toward another sentient being, and the motivation for our actions is rooted in bodhicitta, then even in times of aggression we can still attain enlightenment, because our activities are uncontaminated by any affliction. With genuine bodhicitta in our mind, we do not hope for any return for our deeds, such as wanting to gain any wealth or fame in return as a reward for practicing generosity. Just as the sun and the moon benefit the world spontaneously and have no concept of "What would be good for me?," in the same way, our genuine bodhicitta is not tainted by the hope for any return. Rather, our mind is imbued with pure wishes to spontaneously benefit all sentient beings.

Throughout each of the realms and in every direction,
May I pacify all suffering of the unfortunate realms.
May I establish all beings in happiness,
And may I be of assistance to every one.

In this stanza we pray particularly for the beings of the lower realms—for those in the hell realms, the hungry ghost realms, and the animal realms. With the strong desire to liberate them from the lower existences and to make them understand clearly the reasons that compelled them to descend into those unfortunate existences, we develop love, compassion, and bodhicitta.

Two of the main disciples of Buddha Śākyamuni, Śāriputra and Maudgalyāyana, were such practitioners. Śāriputra is well known for his knowledge and bodhicitta, whereas Maudgalyāyana is known for his extraordinary powers. When Maudgalyāyana went down to the hot hells to try to benefit the beings there, the cool rain that he generated through his miraculous powers did not manage to be of any comfort to the beings there, because it immediately heated up and transformed into hot water. However, Śāriputra, through his bodhicitta and the combination of skillful means, wisdom, and the power of his meditative absorption, was able to bring about a cool rain that brought relief and comfort to all the beings of the hot hells. This story illustrates that bodhicitta is the foundation of any desire to help other sentient beings.

Another example, that of the future Buddha Maitreya, shows that bodhicitta and skillful means go beyond

44

our imagination. It is said that when the human lifespan has decreased to about ten years only—now it is about hundred years—Maitreya will come to this world and manifest as a one-foot tall being to liberate all sentient beings in saṃsāra. Possessing a vast accumulation of merit, one wonders why Maitreya would choose to manifest as such a small being. Maitreya said that manifesting this one-foot tall being was the resultant positive karma of having practiced the ten virtues. Moreover, his body will be magnificent, whereas everybody else will suffer a body of poor health and little beauty. Therefore, those beings will curiously inquire as to how he obtained such an attractive body. Upon hearing the reason, they will feel inspired to practice virtue and accumulate wholesome karma themselves. This story demonstrates that there are all kinds of skillful means to liberate beings from cyclic existence and to help them attain the states of an arhat, pratyekabuddha, or fully enlightened buddha.

May I perfect the practice of enlightened conduct
In accord with the various lifestyles of beings.
May I fully exemplify excellent conduct,
And continue to do so during all future eons.

Practitioners of the bodhisattva way develop different means to benefit beings as they progress along the path of the ten pāramitās. Because of their vast accumulation of merit and wisdom, they can benefit a great number of sentient beings in all the different realms, in accordance with beings' requirements and different needs. Such practitioners excel in untiring perseverance, not disturbed by petty thoughts such as, "There are too many sentient beings who need to be liberated," or, "It will take too long," or, "They have accumulated too much bad karma which makes it too hard to liberate them."

Buddha Amitābha exemplifies such excellent bodhicitta, which has three aspects to it: the promise to persevere toward buddhahood regardless of the time required, regardless of the number of sentient beings in saṃsāra, and regardless of how difficult it might be to help all of them. It is because of such pure aspiration of Buddha Amitābha that we have the pure land of Great Bliss— also called *Dewachen*, or *Sukhāvatī*. It is the most auspicious of the pure lands, because even we human beings can obtain a rebirth in Dewachen. Whereas other pure realms can be attained solely through the power of realization, Sukhāvatī is the only pure realm that can be accessed on the basis of devotion to Amitābha.

An important aspect of the bodhisattva's work is that benefiting sentient beings has to happen according to their needs, their requirements, and their abilities. Guru Rinpoche (Padmasambhava), for instance, so as to liberate the beings of the rakṣasa-demon realm, manifested himself as that kind of rakṣasa. Emulating the Buddhas of the past, our actions should be in accordance with the needs and requirements of others.

May I always be accompanied by those friends
Whose practice and conduct resemble my own.

With regard to our body, speech, and mind,
May all of our actions and prayers be as one.

Dharma friends give us immense support as we go along the bodhisattva's practice path. If we have positive Dharma friends who accompany us and who aid and guide us, this support helps remove many obstacles, as well as ensures that we are not negatively inf luenced by unwholesome friends to deviate from the correct path. Our practice is complete when it encompasses the three aspects of our being: with our body we continuously practice generosity and the other pāramitās; with our speech we regularly study, express, and recite the Dharma; and with our mind we think constantly about bodhicitta and all the accumulations we can generate.

May I always encounter companions
Who exemplify excellent conduct
And have my well-being at heart.
May I never let these teachers down.

Once upon a time, there was a buddha who gave teachings on the universe and the pure realms. He was called Dramdze Gyatso, which means "ocean of saints," and had one thousand disciples to whom he taught the Dharma and gave refuge. After mastering the path, each disciple selected one of the worlds to go to and liberate sentient beings. All worlds were accommodated, except for one—the human world, at the time of one hundred years life expectancy. None of those one thousand disciples volunteered to liberate humans, since humans were generally considered too barbaric, too deeply-rooted in their negative karma to be tamed or taught, and simply too difficult. Finally, the teacher himself took on the responsibility to liberate humans in this samsaric world. That teacher was none other than our teacher, Buddha Śākyamuni. This story is an example of how important it is to have Dharma friends along the way who are willing to help and to guide us as we progress along the practice path of a bodhisattva.

Having understood how important it is to have genuine teachers and companions, we should do our practice with gratitude, and meet the expectations of our teachers, whatever they may be. Take, for example, the great Dharma Lord Gampopa, who followed his master, Milarepa, in an exemplary manner. Gampopa is one of those masters who had been prophesied by Buddha Śākyamuni. This prophecy can be found in the *Samādhirāja Sūtra*. Gampopa developed strong faith the very first time he heard his guru Milarepa's name. Based on his exceptional faith and pure dedication, within seventeen days of practice after having met his guru, he achieved a high level of spontaneous meditative absorption power. This result was enabled by the vast amount of bodhicitta he had generated prior to his meeting Milarepa, as well as by the strong unswerving faith that he had for his guru. We should emulate the example of Gampopa and follow in his footsteps to ensure that we encounter our guru, that we encounter the Dharma, and that we do our best to fulfill the teacher's expectations.

May I always directly perceive the victorious ones:
The protectors and their entourage of bodhisattvas.

In this stanza we make dedicated wishes to always be in the presence and directly perceive the Buddhas, together with their retinues of arhats, pratyekabuddhas, and bodhisattvas, in order to emulate their accomplishments, and to be able to transform all outer phenomena into pure realms. Although such achievements are only possible for practitioners on the tenth bhūmi and beyond, or for those who have attained the three kāyas of buddhahood, the ordinary practitioner nevertheless plants the seeds now for similar results in the future.

Throughout all future eons, may I never grow weary
Of honoring them with remarkably vast offerings.

As sincere practitioners, we should not become weary or hesitant in our perseverance to train and purify our mind, even if it may take many eons. Furthermore, we have to transcend concepts of length of time, of quantity, or size. We simply continually envisage all the buddha realms in all the most subtle atoms, we make offerings, pay homage, and request buddhas to turn the wheel of Dharma and to remain until ultimate enlightenment is reached. In the context of the Vajrayāna it is taught that it is possible to accomplish enlightenment within one lifetime only. This exceptional result has been produced by the best of practitioners who generated the power of genuine bodhicitta, without ever becoming victims of weariness or depression.

May I uphold the genuine Dharma of the buddhas,
And make enlightened conduct fully manifest.
May I be perfectly trained in excellent conduct,
Wholeheartedly continuing for eons to come.

Just like the great bodhisattva Mañjuśrī, who received vast amounts of teachings from all the past buddhas and practiced them, we also commit to memory all the Dharma teachings, such as the six pāramitās, and bring them to accomplishment for the sake of all sentient beings. Thus, we follow in his footsteps and vow to do so for all our future lifetimes, for eons to come.

Through all my existences, be they within saṃsāra,
May I acquire inexhaustible merit and wisdom.
May these become a never-ending treasure of qualities:
Methods, superior knowledge, samādhi, and liberation.

The accumulation of merit, and the power that is generated along the bodhisattva path, are the subject of this stanza. Merit and power lead to three main achievements: skillful methods, superior knowledge, and *samādhi*, or the power of meditative absorption.

Remember the story of the Buddha's two main disciples, Śāriputra and Maudgalyāyana, who went to the hot hells to save all hell beings there. They used these three kinds of powers—skillful means, wisdom and samādhi—in order to be of benefit to those suffering beings. In the same way, we also have to develop powers and qualities which will enable us to truly benefit beings. Although bodhisattva trainees may require three eons before they can accomplish total enlightenment and master all corresponding powers, nevertheless they make sure their conduct is uncontaminated all along and their motivation is rooted in bodhicitta.

Atop one particle, there are as many realms as atoms;
In each pure realm, more buddhas than can be imagined
Reside amidst bodhisattvas, their spiritual heirs.
May I see them and emulate their enlightened activity.

This verse serves as a reminder of our visualization and our understanding. The power of pure aspiration is based on a practitioner's realization of the three spheres, that is, the emptiness of self, the emptiness of other, and the emptiness of the relation that exists between the two. This understanding is the underlying basis of a vast and powerful accumulation. Moreover, this stanza recalls the visualization of one single atom filled with countless buddha realms, which are not crowded despite the fact that they exist on one tiny particle. Within each realm a buddha resides with his entourage of bodhisattvas, arhats, and pratyekabuddhas. This visualization is expressed repeatedly throughout the prayer and the teachings because it is such an important method that combines bodhicitta with the realization of the emptiness of the three spheres, thereby generating immense merit.

Likewise, in absolutely every direction,
Within the space on the tip of one hair,
There are oceans of buddhas of past, present, and future,

Oceans of pure realms and oceans of eons.
May I fully take part in this enlightened activity.

This stanza again emphasizes the importance of transforming outer phenomena into pure lands in all ten directions, as well as the importance of always emulating the examples of the buddhas in their total accomplishment. Once more we are reminded to abandon the worldly concept of largeness or smallness by contemplating that within a very minute amount of space, like the tip of a hair, the manifestation of all the buddhas of the three times—past, present, and future—can take place. The word "ocean," which occurs frequently throughout the whole prayer, refers to how countless and immeasurable these pure lands and buddhas are.

The sound of one instance of the Buddha's speech,
With its ocean of qualities, holds the pure range
Of harmonious expressions of all victorious ones;
It is the very melody of each being's understanding.
May I always engage in the speech of the buddhas.

This stanza refers to the meritorious power of speech, which is generated by bodhisattva practice. The buddhas' speech is pure and complete, and endowed with special powers. One single sound of a buddha's speech embodies simultaneously the whole range of languages, tones, and expressions that various sentient beings require to understand reality and be liberated. The speech of buddhas is aptly suited to every maturity level of sentient beings, wherever they may be and in whichever realm they might reside. With this verse, the practitioner aspires to practice the bodhisattva path until he or she has obtained these meritorious powers of speech, as complete and pure as those which the buddhas have accomplished in the past.

All victorious ones of past, present, and future
Fully turn the wheel of Dharma in a variety of ways.
Through the power of mind, may I also participate
In the boundless expression of their melodious speech.

This verse refers to the turning of the wheel of Dharma. In our samsaric world, Buddha Śākyamuni turned the wheel of Dharma three times. The first turning of the Dharma wheel consisted of the teaching of the "Four Noble Truths." In the second turning of the Dharma wheel, the Buddha taught the "Lack of Characteristics," and the third is the final turning of the Dharma wheel of "Fine Distinctions." All these teachings of the three turnings of the Dharma wheel were collected conscientiously by the Buddha's main disciple, Śāriputra. He also stated to whom, and to what level of sentient beings, the Buddha was explaining these Dharma teachings. In this stanza, the practitioner aspires to emulate the example of Śāriputra and wishes to commit to memory and assemble all the vast teachings of the Buddhas without any inaccuracy or fault.

In a single instant, may I engage in
All future eons which will be experienced.
In just a split second, may I take part in
Any and all of the eons of the three times.

At the moment of completely perfect enlightenment, a bodhisattva masters two different kinds of wisdom. The first of these is the wisdom of knowing all phenomena, the second one is the all-accomplishing wisdom. The first of these is the wisdom that knows in one instant all phenomena of the past, present, and future. Buddha Śākyamuni foretold, for instance, the coming of Nāgārjuna, which happened about five hundred years after his passing. He foretold very clearly Nāgārjuna's practice, his habits, and even aspects of his consciousness; he foretold when he would attain the first bhūmi, and the causes for that accomplishment. He foretold which types of bodhisattvas were going to be in Nāgārjuna's entourage of disciples. He also prophesied in detail which particular practices and Mādhyamaka teachings Nāgārjuna would expound. This is an example of the wisdom of knowing all phenomena in one instant.

A buddha knows the total complete range of cause and effect in all the future times. How can somebody, in one split second, take part in all eons of the three times— past, present, and future? The power of this wisdom of knowing all phenomena is rooted in the non-differential equality of the three times. A Buddha realizes that there is no difference between the three times, as time is just a fabricated concept. This realization generates the wisdom of knowing all phenomena. With this stanza, practitioners aspire to possess the same power of the wisdom of all phenomena. The all-accomplishing wisdom will be explained below.

In the space of a single moment, may I behold
All lions among men of past, present, and future.
May I continually engage in their field of experience
Through the power of illusion-like spiritual liberation.

The prayer continues with the wish to partake in the vast activity of the buddhas of the three times. Buddhas do not act by deliberately deciding, "I will do this and that, or I should do this and that." Quite the opposite, their realization of the three spheres' emptiness implies there being no attachment involved at all. Their entire activity is performed spontaneously. Buddha activity does not exist as a solid reality; thus, it is free to manifest in an illusory manner for the spiritual liberation of all beings. The practitioners of the bodhisattva path make the wish to perfect this kind of enlightened activity.

The clusters of galaxies of past, present, and future
Have all been established atop a single particle.
Accordingly, in all directions, without exception,
May I take part in the pure realms of the victors.

This stanza refers to the aforementioned miraculous power to benefit sentient beings through the manifestation of buddha realms. Buddha Amitābha manifested the pure realm of Sukhāvatī, or Dewachen, by the power of his profound aspiration. He thereby enabled ordinary beings to attain rebirth in a pure realm where they could continue their Dharma practice in the most conducive environment. Likewise, practitioners of the bodhisattva path make the wish to be able to manifest similar buddha realms, and this wish is not limited to a single pure realm. Instead, it is as vast as the universe itself, including every single atom in it.

The lanterns of the world who have yet to come
Will all, by stages, become fully enlightened,
Turn the wheel of the Dharma, and demonstrate
The state beyond suffering, ultimate peace.
May I be in the presence of all those protectors.

This stanza describes the activity of the numerous bodhisattvas of the future who will attain completely perfect enlightenment, as well as the practitioners' wish to partake in their activity. Just as the gods of the heavenly realms made offerings to Buddha Śākyamuni, the practitioners make offerings to all future buddhas and also promise to support them.

Buddha Śākyamuni accomplished twelve specific actions in his lifetime. Similarly, the future buddhas will display these "Twelve Deeds of the Buddha." They include, among others, his descent from Tuṣita; the conception and birth; his training in the arts, crafts, and sciences; his marriage; his renunciation; his asceticism; his victory over *māra*; his enlightenment under the bodhi tree in Bodh Gayā; teaching the Dharma in Vārāṇasī and elsewhere; up until his passing away into parinirvāṇa to teach perfect full awakening. His disciple Ānanda supported Buddha Śākyamuni throughout the majority of these twelve events. The practitioners aspire with this verse to be in the presence of a buddha, and taking Ānanda as an example, they wish to serve the future buddhas throughout their twelve deeds of enlightenment.

This verse is of special importance for yet another reason. During the time of the 14th Karmapa, in the beginning of the nineteenth century, a group of lamas of the Nyingma Mindrolling Monastery were invited to Tsurphu Monastery, the main seat of the Karmapas in Tibet, to perform a lengthy ritual of Dorje Phurba.

The Mindrolling lamas had the habit of reciting the *Noble King of Prayers of Excellent Conduct* up to the last line of this stanza. Here they stopped very briefly to pay homage to Master Dharma Śri, who had been captured about a century earlier, when the Mongolian army invaded the country and destroyed a great number of Buddhist reliquaries and monasteries in Tibet, including Mindrolling Monastery. When they captured Master Dharma Śri, they tied him to a horse tail and dragged him around on the open ground. The master kept on reciting the *Noble King of Prayers of Excellent Conduct*, and upon reaching this particular line, he passed away. Therefore, it became a practice in future generations of practitioners to stop momentarily in the recitation at this point, in remembrance of this great master who did not lose his bodhicitta in the face of cruelty. Also, in our Kagyu tradition, we have adopted this manner of paying homage to a man who displayed inconceivably great bodhicitta. He is an example of a bodhisattva who transformed a situation of suffering into the perfection of tolerance.

By virtue of the powers of miraculous swiftness,
The powers of the manifold approaches of the yānas,

The powers of practice endowed with all qualities,
The powers of omnipresent lovingkindness,
The powers of perfectly virtuous goodness,
The powers of unbounded timeless wisdom,
The powers of knowledge, means, and deep meditation,
May I truly achieve the many powers of awakening.

Bodhisattvas develop particular powers as they progress along the five paths and the ten bhūmis toward enlightenment. The techniques with which practitioners achieve these powers are the practices of *śamatha* and *vipaśyanā*.

The first of these powers is the power of miraculous swiftness with which all the Buddhas of the different Buddha realms accomplish their activity. The second is the power of *yāna*. This Sanskrit word *yāna* means "vehicle." Here it refers specifically to the *Mahāyāna*, and implies the meaning of support for the practitioner on the path to enlightenment. The yāna is the support via which the practitioner achieves the ultimate goal. The third power is the power of merit which refers to all the bodhisattva qualities and merits in which all beings, even those of the lower realms, such as animals, can rejoice. The fourth is the power of lovingkindness. This power is brought about by the four immeasurable thoughts—love, compassion, sympathetic joy, and equanimity—the root of which is *samādhi*, or meditative absorption. The power of perfectly virtuous goodness is derived from the pāramitā of generosity. By giving away possessions and wealth, granting protection, and by spreading the Dharma teaching, this power of goodness is accumulated. The power of wisdom is what causes you to be ultimately free from any worldly boundaries, such as defilement or attachment. The power of skillful means is achieved through a combination of knowledge and meditation. The power of samādhi enables the practitioner to perceive the emptiness of all illusory phenomena. A bodhisattva on the tenth bhūmi who is familiar with the "vajra meditative absorption" has obtained this particular power. It is the very level of meditative absorption, or samādhi, that Buddha Śākyamuni achieved under the bodhi tree in Bodh Gayā. The term *vajra* means indestructible, and indicates that this meditative absorption has overcome and destroyed all the obstacles of the path, particularly the obstacle caused by conceptual knowledge.

May I completely purify the powers of karma,
Fully defeat the powers of the afflictions,
Utterly disable the powers of the māras,
And bring the power of excellent conduct to perfection.

Not only does the practitioner develop powers; obstacles have their innate power, too. The combination of skillful means and wisdom acts as an antidote to obstructing powers. There are three different kinds of obstacles to our samādhi, the first of which is the obstacle of karma, the second is the obstacle of mental afflictions (*kleśa*), and the third is the obstacle of *māra*.

Karma is like a contaminated seed being planted into our stream of consciousness. It grows in the soil of ignorance and produces the dualistic mode of perception that we are all used to, which leads us to sow further negative karma, again reinforcing the imprints planted in our mind. The obstacle of karma constitutes the cause for rebirth in cyclic existence, characterized by suffering. How do we apply an antidote to the obstacle of karma? The practitioner has to engage in the accumulation of positive karma, that is, meritorious deeds. Moreover, genuine positive karma is generated by realizing the essence of mind, that is, the emptiness of self. Once this realization is firmly established, the contaminated seeds have no more ground for sprouting or growing.

The second obstacle, the obstacle of mental afflictions, is derived from ego-clinging. Because of ego-clinging, emotions such as greed, hatred, jealousy, envy, and so on, can develop. These in turn compel us to commit all kinds of negative activities. The only complete antidote for overcoming these mental afflictions is the realization of selflessness.

The third obstacle is called the obstacle of *māra*. There are four types of māra, namely the *kleśa-māra*, which is the māra of mental afflictions; second, the *skandha-māra*, which refers to the attachment to our psycho-physical aggregates; third is the *māra of death*; and fourth is the *devaputra-māra*, which is the māra of spiritual pride.

May I totally purify oceans of realms,
Entirely liberate oceans of beings,
Clearly behold oceans of Dharma,

Wholly integrate oceans of wisdom,
Patently clarify oceans of conduct,
Perfectly fulfill oceans of aspirations,
Honor oceans of buddhas with my offerings,
And practice tirelessly during oceans of eons.

This stanza illustrates the variety of activities that a practitioner emulating the buddhas will perform. What are buddhas' activities? They are actions accomplished exclusively for the benefit of sentient beings. What are the sources of buddhas' activities? They are derived from a combination of the power of aspiration, as well as miraculous powers, skillful means, and samādhi. Obtaining these is the result of diligent practice.

Bodhisattvas have the ability to transform contaminated places into pure Buddha lands. We ordinary beings do not have such capacities since we have accumulated a vast amount of emotional afflictions (kleśa) and their resultant negative karma with our body, speech, and mind; these obstruct our attempts to be of real benefit to beings. On our practice path toward ultimate enlightenment, we need to purify our negative karma by means of the various skillful methods that the Buddha taught in accordance with different types of sentient beings.

As mentioned above, a buddha possesses two aspects of wisdom: the wisdom of knowing all phenomena, and the all-accomplishing wisdom. This stanza makes reference to both these aspects, thereby illustrating the limitless ways in which buddhas accomplish the benefit of sentient beings. Since the wisdom of knowing all phenomena has already been explained, here it is appropriate to briefly explain the all-accomplishing wisdom. Buddhas can manifest in multiple forms to help beings overcome their difficulties, and they choose the most inconceivable and efficient methods. Like a doctor analyzing a patient and then offering the best available treatment, the buddhas understand spontaneously what sentient beings need and manifest it effortlessly and perfectly. For the sick, they themselves become the medicine, or the doctor, that will cure their diseases.

We practitioners make aspirations accordingly. In order to attain that level of realization, we first of all join in the aspirations of all buddhas and pray sincerely that these be perfectly fulfilled; moreover, we honor oceans of buddhas with offerings, vowing to practice tirelessly for oceans of eons.

Once I have awakened and attained buddhahood
By means of the practice of excellent conduct,
May I fulfill all special wishes of enlightened conduct
Expressed by victorious ones of past, present and future.

By following the example of the buddhas of the three times of past, present, and future, and by generating bodhicitta and applying ourselves diligently to the bodhisattva path, we practitioners traverse the five paths and the ten bhūmis until we reach the final result of buddhahood. Then, we will be able to benefit beings through the two form kāyas: Sublime beings are benefited through the saṃbhogakāya form, and ordinary beings through the nirmāṇakāya form. We

make prayers to manifest as many saṃbhogakāya
and nirmāṇakāya forms as necessary to benefit all
sentient beings.

The eldest son of the victorious ones
Is known as Samantabhadra, the All-Excellent.
In order to equal his masterful skill,
I perfectly dedicate all forms of merit.
May I be comparable to Samantabhadra:
His utterly pure body, speech, and mind,
His totally pure conduct, perfectly pure realms,
And superior skill in dedicating merit.

These eight lines summarize in five key points the
entirety of Samantabhadra's aspirations. The first
one refers to the body. His utterly pure body can
manifest in as many different forms as possible for the
benefit of all sentient beings. The second is related
to his speech, which is active in as many ways as
necessary to benefit a multitude of sentient beings.
The third one refers to his mind, which is free from
greed, ego-clinging, and any expectation of receiving
something in return for his acts of generosity, or for
his practice in general. The fourth key characteristic
is his totally correct bodhisattva conduct which
consists of the practice of the six perfections, or
pāramitās, that generate the corresponding powers
to effortlessly remove all obstacles that might hinder
bodhisattva practice. The fifth key point refers to his
ability to transform contaminated phenomena into
completely pure buddha fields. These five different
key points combined describe Samantabhadra's

profound aspirations, which have been praised and are continuously commended by past and present buddhas.

So as to completely achieve excellent goodness,
I will carry out Mañjuśrī's aspiration prayers.
Continuing tirelessly throughout future eons,
I will accomplish every last one of his activities.

This stanza refers to Bodhisattva Mañjuśrī's aspirations, which have to be understood as complementary to Bodhisattva Samantabhadra's aspiration, since both bodhisattvas are considered equally important heart disciples of the Buddha.

In one of his previous lifetimes, Bodhisattva Mañjuśrī told King Namka, "Until all beings reach enlightenment, I will be a bodhisattva." This doesn't mean that Mañjuśrī is not a buddha. Mañjuśrī primarily made a promise to himself, pledging that he will be a bodhisattva and act compassionately as long as beings exist. He generated such strong, genuine bodhicitta that he wished for all sentient beings to be liberated from suffering without a single exception. Here the question may arise: When will the time arrive where no sentient being is left to be liberated?

Rather than looking outside to inquire about sentient beings out there who are yet to be liberated, we should turn inward and look into our own heart and motivation. We ask ourselves, have I abandoned greed and desire to benefit sentient beings? We aspire to become like Mañjuśrī, who never lost the desire to benefit sentient beings, and who never lost the bodhicitta that he had generated. Likewise, we protect our bodhicitta in our hearts, as well as our desire to benefit all countless beings. Moreover, we must be free from attachment and from hope for a reward.

From Śāntideva's *Bodhicaryāvatāra*, we read in Chapter Three:

> *For sentient beings, poor and destitute,*
> *May I become a treasure ever plentiful,*
> *And lie before them closely in their reach,*
> *And varied source of all that they might need.*
> *My body thus, and all my goods besides,*
> *And all my merits gained and to be gained,*
> *I give them all away withholding nothing*
> *To bring about the benefit of beings.* [3.10-11]

In other words, we are saying: "When practicing the generosity pāramitā, I want to give all my possessions for the benefit of all beggars." Does this mean that we keep on giving until there are no more beggars to be found? It does not. Rather, Śāntideva communicates the attitude to adopt: We give our possessions wholeheartedly and with a mind free from the defilement of attachment, never losing sight of that desire to relieve beggars from suffering. That is the practice of the generosity pāramitā.

Likewise, does the pāramitā of ethical conduct mean that we will practice life release daily forever, continuously releasing birds or fish and so on? Again, no. Rather, the practice consists of generating the wish in our heart to release life wherever and whenever we can and never discarding that wish.

Furthermore, it includes wishing never to cause harm to another sentient being, to the extent of giving up our own body for the sake of others. In brief, we do not need to take into consideration how long a time or how much effort will be required to benefit beings. Instead, we concentrate on the quality of our aspiration. Such is the way to emulate the aspiration and the activities of the Bodhisattva Mañjuśrī.

May my actions be free of limitations,
And my qualities also be without bounds.
May I remain engaged in activities beyond measure,
And may I come to know all of their manifestations.

This stanza emphasizes again the limitless character of a bodhisattva's aspiration power that we wish to generate when we follow the example of Samantabhadra. The accumulation of such aspiration power is truly without limit.

There are countless beings, as limitless
As the very confines of the endless sky.
Whatever their karma and afflictions may be,
May my wishing prayers encompass them all.

This verse also illustrates the infinite character of true aspiration. As bodhisattvas, our aspiration shall be beyond boundaries and shall have no limit, just like the sky. Where the sky exists, different realms and worlds exist. And where worlds exist, sentient beings also exist, immersed in their particular suffering. So bodhisattva path practitioners aspire to have their accumulated power of bodhicitta be infinite like the sky in order to benefit all the countless beings in the limitless realms.

Benefits of Practicing
Samantabhadra's Wishing Prayer

**We may embellish the infinite realms of the ten directions
With precious gems and present them to the victorious ones;
We may offer the finest pleasures of gods and humans
During as many eons as there are atoms in the universe.
Even so, paramount indeed is the exceptional merit
Of those of us who have heard this King of Dedications,
Are truly determined to pursue supreme enlightenment,
And give rise to genuine faith, be it just for a moment.**

These verses refer to the limitless benefits that are generated when we follow the example of Samantabhadra's aspiration. If, in the infinite realms of the ten directions, one were to manifest multiple riches and all the finest and most precious heavenly and worldly treasures and offer them to the buddhas, the generated merit would be, of course, immeasurable. If one were to continue to do so for many eons, the accumulated merit would be unfathomable. However, compared to one who recites the *Noble King of Prayers of Excellent Conduct* and generates the aspiration power accordingly, the merit generated from this practice is far greater than that accrued by making all these material offerings.

Those who practice this Prayer of Excellent Conduct
Will turn away from rebirth in the lower realms,
Sever all ties to unwholesome companions,
And promptly behold Amitābha, Infinite Light.

The recitation of this prayer has the power to eliminate the negative karma that would lead to a rebirth in the lower realms of the hells, hungry ghosts, or animals. Instead, you will attain a precious rebirth as a human or god, and continuously proceed on the path of a bodhisattva. And you will come to meet with the Buddhadharma, be in the companionship of Dharma friends, and be protected from all kinds of evil influences or companions that would lead you to the lower realms.

The following story illustrates the harm that evil companions can inflict. There was a king during Buddha Śākyamuni's time called Ajātaśatru. This king, although a sponsor of Buddha Śākyamuni, was cheated and influenced by his companions who belonged to a sect of evil-minded fellows. Those were followers of Devadatta, Buddha's cousin, whose mind was set on causing harm to the Dharma. Even though this king initially had good intentions, he came under disastrous influence and engaged in negative activities that harmed his practice.

On the other hand, when we practice the *Noble King of Prayers of Excellent Conduct* wholeheartedly, we are certain to take rebirth in Dewachen, the pure land of Amitābha, where we will meet the Buddha of Infinite Light face to face.

They will be perfectly comfortable and lead happy lives;
In this lifetime as well, comfort and happiness will reign.
Without delay, they will become similar in every way
To Samantabhadra, the All-Excellent One.

A further benefit of practicing the aspirations of Samantabhadra is that we will attain a precious human rebirth, be in the company of good Dharma companions, and accumulate causes and positive karma that help us to eliminate any negativities and obstacles that will hinder our practice along the bodhisattva path. Just as Samantabhadra overcame all these obstacles that hindered his practice path, so will the practitioner of his prayer be guided along in the same manner.

If this Prayer of Excellent Conduct is recited
By those who have committed, by reason of ignorance,
The five most negative acts of direct consequence,
These all will be quickly and thoroughly purified.

This stanza mentions the five most negative acts of direct consequence. One should have no doubt that the grave negative karmic consequences brought about by these negative acts can be overcome by the practice of the *Noble King of Prayers of Excellent Conduct.*

What are these five negative acts? They are killing one's father, killing one's mother, killing an arhat, breaking up the harmony of the Saṃgha (the monastic community of the Buddha), and hurting or harming the Buddha. These are not hypothetical cases; these acts have been committed countless times. The negativity of these acts is particularly grave, because, for instance, our parents are the people to whom we are most indebted for bringing us into this world and raising us. Killing them would therefore, be one of the five most negative acts one can imagine. An arhat is an accomplished practitioner and a source of refuge for sentient beings. Therefore, it is an extremely negative act to kill an arhat. To use slander, lies, or conspiracy to disrupt the harmony of the Saṃgha which spreads the Buddha's teachings is another inexcusable act. As for attacking and harming the Buddha, this is obviously an act of extreme aggression, and therefore of immense negative consequences.

At the time of Buddha Śākyamuni, his cousin Devadatta, together with king Ajātaśatru, planned to cause great harm to the Dharma by breaking up the Saṃgha into two conflicting parties through conspiracy and slander. Devadatta was in the grip of agonizing jealousy and aversion toward the Buddha, envying his accomplishments and qualities. So much so that on one occasion he threw a stone to hit the Buddha and hurt the Buddha's foot. But even though all these negative acts would potentially lead to an immediate rebirth in the lower realms after death, if with regret and sincerity the person were to practice Samantabhadra's aspirations, the great consequences and negative results could be eliminated.

Practitioners will have wisdom, the shapeliest physique, Excellent signs, a noble family, and a fine complexion.

**The many māras and heretics will be powerless
  against them,
And they will be honored throughout the three worlds.**

The practice of the *Noble King of Prayers of Excellent Conduct* does not only avert obstructions, it will lead moreover to countless favorable results, such as expressed in this verse. Practitioners will be so rich in merit that their physical appearance will be like that of divine beings of the heavenly realms, endowed with fine complexion and exquisite beauty. They will be born into a noble family, display excellent signs, and so on, and will possess enough wisdom to benefit all sentient beings. Potential obstacles created by māra, as was explained previously, cannot hinder the practice of these practitioners.

In the spiritual world, there are a number of groups that can have, in a more or less obvious way, negative influences on their followers. In the long term such practitioners transform gradually into unwholesome people, and are influenced to engage in distorted ways of thinking. All these obstacles can be safely removed through the wishing prayers of Samantabhadra.

A genuine practitioner of the bodhisattva path generates aspiration powers simply by following the example of Samantabhadra. By doing so, he or she will be praised by all beings in all the three realms whether they are beings of the heavenly realms or the lower realms, even the hell realms. How is that possible? Śāntideva mentions in the *Bodhicaryāvatāra* that even beings in the hell realms would have a chance to come face to face with bodhisattvas such as Vajrapani, Mañjuśrī, and Avalokiteśvara because of the power of these bodhisattvas' aspirations. Beings in the hells have no other hope than relying on the aspiration powers generated by these great bodhisattvas so as to be able to witness them. It is part of a bodhisattva's courageous commitment to help beings everywhere without exception; and the courageous practitioners who emulate the great bodhisattvas are themselves worthy of praise.

They will go quickly before the great bodhi tree,
And settle there for the benefit of sentient beings.
As awakened buddhas they will turn the wheel of Dharma,
Prevailing against all of the māras and their legions.

According to ancient predictions, in our current fortunate kalpa, one thousand buddhas will appear. Four of these buddhas attained enlightenment under the great bodhi tree. In fact, six buddhas have already manifested in our era, but among those six, the first two did not attain enlightenment in this present world. Therefore, only four of the buddhas attained enlightenment under the bodhi tree.

The buddhas of the past have all manifested the Twelve Deeds of the Buddha. Just as Buddha Śākyamuni did, they gave up worldly pleasures, they dedicated their lives to the practice path, overcame all the temptations and obstacles of māra, attained enlightenment, and turned the wheel of Dharma for the benefit of all sentient beings. In the same way that the past buddhas have manifested in this world and attained enlightenment, we pray with these recitations that all future buddhas will attain enlightenment under the bodhi tree and continue to turn the wheel of Dharma for the benefit of all sentient beings.

The buddhas alone fathom the full karmic fruition
For those who take this Prayer of Excellent Activity
To heart by expounding it, or reading and reciting it.
Have no doubt: the outcome is supreme awakening!

As practitioners we should dispel any doubts that we might have about the vast and immense power and merit accumulated with this *Noble King of Prayers of Excellent Conduct.* The full extent of such powers cannot be understood by normal human beings or beings who are still on the path toward enlightenment. Only buddhas can fully conceive of the complete range of benefits and merit powers when all these aspirations practices come to fruition.

THE PRAYER —DEDICATION

May I train by emulating the examples of Mañjuśrī,
With his momentous knowledge and great courage,
And Samantabhadra, whose qualities are identical;
Like them, I perfectly dedicate all forms of merit.
For the sake of the practice of excellent conduct,
I completely dedicate all of my roots of goodness

By means of those dedications praised as supreme
By the victorious ones of past, present, and future.

This is the dedication of merit for the sake of all sentient beings. The first four lines indicate how we dedicate the merit by following the example of bodhisattvas, in particular Mañjuśrī and Samantabhadra. With the last four lines we join our dedication of merit with that of the buddhas of the past, present, and future. Just as they have dedicated their accomplishments and merits for the benefit of all sentient beings alike, we do the same—we simply follow the example of the buddhas of the three times.

When the time has come for me to die,
And all of my veils, now purified, disappear,
May I directly behold Amitābha, Infinite Light,
And proceed with certainty to the realm of joy.

In addition to dedicating the merit, there is a special wish for oneself and all beings to take rebirth in Dewachen, the pure land of Buddha Amitābha. This wish implies that all sentient beings shall be reborn in the pure realm without having to go through the experiences of the bardo. There shall be no obstacles and no veils of negative karma. Instead, at the moment of death, when we have to depart from this life, we shall come directly face to face with the Buddha Amitābha, the Buddha of Infinite Light, and proceed with certainty to be reborn in the realm of joy, his pure land, Dewachen.

Once there, may these and all other prayers,
Without a single exception, become manifest.
May I perfectly fulfill each and every one,
Helping beings for as long as the universe exists.

Once we have taken rebirth in Dewachen, the pure land of Buddha Amitābha, we wish that all our prayers be completely fulfilled in their totality, and that consequently the endless cycles of sentient beings' suffering be removed. This is part of the major aspiration for being reborn in Dewachen.

May I be reborn in a supremely beautiful lotus
In the excellent, joyous mandala of the buddhas.
There, may I obtain my prophetic revelation
Directly from Amitābha, the Victorious One.

Once we have taken rebirth in Dewachen, the accumulation of our merit and wisdom, together with Buddha Amitābha's vast aspiration power, will work together so that there will be no need for us ever to go through a contaminated birth again. We will take a pure birth form in a lotus in Dewachen, and we will obtain a prophetic revelation by Buddha Amitābha that we will attain the first level of bodhisattva practice, that is, the first bhūmi, and that we will continue along the path until complete and perfect buddhahood.

Once the prophecy has been fully achieved,
May I serve the beings of the ten directions
In a number of ways through the power of mind
Of many hundreds times millions of emanations.

Once the prophecy that we have obtained from Buddha Amitābha has been fulfilled, we commit to serving all sentient beings in all ten directions. From the attainment of the first bhūmi onward we obtain the power to benefit beings in a multitude of forms, that is, as emanations who benefit various beings in all the worlds and perform as many activities as are required.

By whatever small merit I may have garnered
By practicing this Prayer of Excellent Activity,
May the meritorious aspirations of sentient beings
All be accomplished in the space of one instant.
By virtue of the boundless, genuine merit
Gained by fully dedicating excellent conduct,
May all beings engulfed in the great river of suffering
Attain Buddha Amitābha's most excellent domain.

These eight lines of dedication focus on the positive aspirations accumulated by all sentient beings, and support them so that they may be accomplished in the same way as Samantabhadra's aspirations. Not only will the wholesome wishes of sentient beings be accomplished, but beings in the lower realms will be liberated from their intense suffering, resulting in the complete dissolution of the lower realms. And all this is entirely due to the vast merit and power of the aspiration.

May these sovereign aspiration prayers
Bring about that which is most excellent and sublime,
And may they benefit all beings, infinite in number.

May this scripture adorned by Samantabhadra be accomplished,
And may the entire space of the unfortunate realms become empty.

This verse concludes the dedication of the roots of merit. The final wish is that all beings of the lower realms may be free from suffering, which means that the lower realms shall be emptied and disappear altogether so that not even the word "suffering" is heard anymore.

This concludes the teachings on the *Noble King of Prayers of Excellent Conduct* by Künzig Shamar Rinpoche in Bodh Gayā, in the winter of 2009.

The Noble King of Aspiration Prayers

Tibetan Text and English Translation

༄༅། །འཕགས་པ་བཟང་པོ་སྤྱོད་པའི་སྨོན་ལམ་གྱི་རྒྱལ་པོ་བཞུགས་སོ།།

The King of Aspiration Prayers
of Noble, Excellent Activity

Translated under the guidance of
Künzig Shamar Rinpoche
by Pamela Gayle White

འཕགས་པ་འཇམ་དཔལ་གཞོན་ནུར་གྱུར་པ་ལ་ཕྱག་འཚལ་ལོ།

pakpa jampel zhönnour gyourpa la chak tsal lo

I bow down before the Noble Youth, Lord Mañjuśrī.

།ཇི་སྙེད་སུ་དག་ཕྱོགས་བཅུའི་འཇིག་རྟེན་ན།
།དུས་གསུམ་གཤེགས་པ་མི་ཡི་སེང་གེ་ཀུན།
།བདག་གིས་མ་ལུས་དེ་དག་ཐམས་ཅད་ལ།
།ལུས་དང་ངག་ཡིད་དང་བས་ཕྱག་བགྱིའོ།

jinyé soudak chok chou'i jikten na
düsoum shékpa miyi sengé kün
dagi malü dédak tamché la
lü tang ngayi dangwé chak gyi-o

།བཟང་པོ་སྤྱོད་པའི་སྨོན་ལམ་སྟོབས་དག་གིས།
།རྒྱལ་བ་ཐམས་ཅད་ཡིད་ཀྱིས་མངོན་སུམ་དུ།
།ཞིང་གི་རྡུལ་སྙེད་ལུས་རབ་བཏུད་པ་ཡིས།
།རྒྱལ་བ་ཀུན་ལ་རབ་ཏུ་ཕྱག་འཚལ་ལོ།

zangpo chöpé mönlam tobdak gi
gyalwa tamché yikyi ngön soum dou
zhingi dülnyé lürab tü pa yi
gyalwa künla rabtou chak tsallo

།རྡུལ་གཅིག་སྟེང་ན་རྡུལ་སྙེད་སངས་རྒྱས་རྣམས།
།སངས་རྒྱས་སྲས་ཀྱི་དབུས་ན་བཞུགས་པ་དག
།དེ་ལྟར་ཆོས་ཀྱི་དབྱིངས་རྣམས་མ་ལུས་པར།
།ཐམས་ཅད་རྒྱལ་བ་དག་གིས་གང་བར་མོས།

dül chik teng na dül nyé sangyé nam
sangyé sékyi üna zhoukpa dak
détar chökyi ying nam malü par
tamché gyalwa dagi gang war mö

In all of the worlds in all ten directions
Reside the tathāgatas of past, present and future.
Before each and every one of these lions among men,
I bow down joyfully with body, speech, and mind.

By the power of wishes of excellent conduct,
Each buddha evoked becomes manifest.
With as many bodies as atoms in the universe,
I bow down deeply to the victorious ones.

Atop one particle, as many buddhas as particles
Are settled amidst bodhisattvas, their spiritual heirs.
Thus dharmadhātu, the entire sphere of being,
Abounds with the buddhas that I have envisioned.

།དེ་དག་བསྔགས་པ་མི་ཟད་རྒྱ་མཚོ་རྣམས།
།དབྱངས་ཀྱི་ཡན་ལག་རྒྱ་མཚོའི་སྒྲ་ཀུན་གྱིས།
།རྒྱལ་བ་ཀུན་གྱི་ཡོན་ཏན་རབ་བརྗོད་ཅིང་།
།བདེ་བར་གཤེགས་པ་ཐམས་ཅད་བདག་གིས་བསྟོད།

dédak ngakpa mizé gyatso nam
yangi yenlak gyatso'i dra kün gyi
gyalwa kün gyi yönten rab jö ching
déwar shékpa tamché dagi tö

།མེ་ཏོག་དམ་པ་ཕྲེང་བ་དམ་པ་དང་།
།སིལ་སྙན་རྣམས་དང་བྱུག་པའི་གདུགས་མཆོག་དང་།
།མར་མེ་མཆོག་དང་བདུག་སྤོས་དམ་པ་ཡིས།
།རྒྱལ་བ་དེ་དག་ལ་ནི་མཆོད་པར་བགྱི།

métok dampa tréngwa dampa tang
silnyen nam tang joukpé douk chok tang
marmé chok tang doukpö dampa yi
gyalwa dédak lani chöpar gyi

།ན་བཟའ་དམ་པ་རྣམས་དང་དྲི་མཆོག་དང་།
།ཕྱེ་མའི་ཕུར་མ་རི་རབ་མཉམ་པ་དང་།
།བཀོད་པ་ཁྱད་པར་འཕགས་པའི་མཆོག་ཀུན་གྱིས།
།རྒྱལ་བ་དེ་དག་ལ་ཡང་མཆོད་པར་བགྱི།

naza dampa nam tang dri chok tang
chémé pourma rirab nyampa tang
köpa kyépar pakpé chok kün gyi
gyalwa dédak lani chö par gyi

Using every tone of a multitude of melodies
I revere them with boundless oceans of acclaim.
Singing the praises of those gone to bliss,
I honor your qualities, O victorious ones.

Sumptuous flowers, beautiful garlands,
Precious parasols, fine cymbals and balms,
Radiant lamps and the most fragrant incense:
I offer them to you, O victorious ones.

Such wonderful arrays, all perfectly presented—
Exquisite apparel and sweet-smelling perfume,
Jars of scented powder piled high like a mountain—
I offer them to you, O victorious ones.

།མཆོད་པ་གང་རྣམས་བླ་མེད་རྒྱ་ཆེ་བ།
།དེ་དག་རྒྱལ་བ་ཐམས་ཅད་ལ་ཡང་མོས།
།བཟང་པོ་སྤྱོད་ལ་དད་པའི་སྟོབས་དག་གིས།
།རྒྱལ་བ་ཀུན་ལ་ཕྱག་འཚལ་མཆོད་པར་བགྱི།

chöpa gangnam lamé gya chéwa
dédak gyalwa tamché la yang mö
zangpo chöla dépé tobdak gi
gyalwa künla chaktsal chöpar gyi

།འདོད་ཆགས་ཞེ་སྡང་གཏི་མུག་དབང་གིས་ནི།
།ལུས་དང་ངག་དང་དེ་བཞིན་ཡིད་ཀྱིས་ཀྱང་།
།སྡིག་པ་བདག་གིས་བགྱིས་པ་ཅི་མཆིས་པ།
།དེ་དག་ཐམས་ཅད་བདག་གིས་སོ་སོར་བཤགས།

döchak zhédang timouk wangi ni
lü tang ngak tang dézhin yikyi kyang
dikpa dagi gyipa chichi pa
dédak tamché dagi sosor shak

།ཕྱོགས་བཅུའི་རྒྱལ་བ་ཀུན་དང་སངས་རྒྱས་སྲས།
།རང་རྒྱལ་རྣམས་དང་སློབ་དང་མི་སློབ་དང་།
།འགྲོ་བ་ཀུན་གྱི་བསོད་ནམས་གང་ལ་ཡང་།
།དེ་དག་ཀུན་གྱི་རྗེས་སུ་བདག་ཡི་རང་།

chok chou'i gyalwa kün tang sangyé sé
rang gyal nam tang lob tang milob tang
drowa kün gyi sönam gang la yang
dédak kün gyi jésou dayi rang

These vast and superlative offerings
Express my confidence in all of the buddhas.
With the strength of conviction in excellent conduct,
I bow and present them to the victorious ones.

Whatever misdeeds I may have committed
Through body and speech, as well as through mind,
All outcomes of passion and anger and ignorance:
I openly disclose each and every one.

I rejoice in each occurrence of merit produced
By buddhas and bodhisattvas of all ten directions,
By pratyekabuddhas, by those training on the path,
By arhats beyond training, and by every single being.

།གང་རྣམས་ཕྱོགས་བཅུའི་འཇིག་རྟེན་སྒྲོན་མ་དག
།བྱང་ཆུབ་རིམ་པར་སངས་རྒྱས་མ་ཆགས་ཉེས།
།མགོན་པོ་དེ་དག་བདག་གིས་ཐམས་ཅད་ལ།
།འཁོར་ལོ་བླ་ན་མེད་པར་བསྐོར་བར་བསྐུལ།

gang nam chok chou'i jikten drönma dak
jangchoub rimpar sangyé ma chak nyé
gönpo dédak dagi tamché la
khorlo lana mépar korwar kül

།མྱ་ངན་འདའ་སྟོན་གང་བཞེད་དེ་དག་ལ།
།འགྲོ་བ་ཀུན་ལ་ཕན་ཞིང་བདེ་བའི་ཕྱིར།
།བསྐལ་པ་ཞིང་གི་རྡུལ་སྙེད་བཞུགས་པར་ཡང་།
།བདག་གིས་ཐལ་མོ་རབ་སྦྱར་གསོལ་བར་བགྱི།

nya ngen datön gangzhé dédak la
drowa künla pen zhing déwé chir
kalpa zhingi dül nyé zhouk par yang
dagi talmo rab jar sölwar gyi

།ཕྱག་འཚལ་བ་དང་མཆོད་ཅིང་བཤགས་པ་དང་།
།རྗེས་སུ་ཡི་རང་བསྐུལ་ཞིང་གསོལ་བ་ཡི།
།དགེ་བ་ཅུང་ཟད་བདག་གིས་ཅི་བསགས་པ།
།ཐམས་ཅད་བདག་གིས་བྱང་ཆུབ་ཕྱིར་བསྔོའོ།

chak tsalwa tang chö ching shakpa tang
jésou yirang kül zhing sölwa yi
géwa choung zé dagi chi sakpa
tamché dagi jangchoub chir ngo-o

O lanterns who illumine worlds in all ten directions,
By way of the progressive stages of awakening
You have become buddhas, free from attachment.
Protectors, I entreat you all: turn the supreme wheel.

Palms joined, I beseech those among you
Who mean to manifest the state beyond suffering:
For as many eons as there are atoms in the universe,
Remain for the welfare and happiness of all beings.

Whatever small merit has been garnered here
Through prostrating, offering and disclosing,
Rejoicing, entreating and beseeching,
I dedicate it all for the sake of enlightenment.

།འདས་པའི་སངས་རྒྱས་རྣམས་དང་ཕྱོགས་བཅུ་ཡི།
།འཇིག་རྟེན་དག་ན་གང་བཞུགས་མཆོད་པར་གྱུར།
།གང་ཡང་མ་བྱོན་དེ་དག་རབ་མྱུར་བར།
།བསམ་རྫོགས་བྱང་ཆུབ་རིམ་པར་སངས་རྒྱས་སྤྱོན།

dépé sangyé nam tang chok chou yi
jikten dak na gang zhouk chöpar gyour
gangyang majön dédak rab nyourwar
sam dzok jangchoub rimpar sangyé jön

།ཕྱོགས་བཅུ་ག་ལའི་ཞིང་རྣམས་ཇི་སྙེད་པ།
།དེ་དག་རྒྱ་ཆེར་ཡོངས་སུ་དག་པར་གྱུར།
།བྱང་ཆུབ་ཤིང་དབང་དྲུང་གཤེགས་རྒྱལ་བ་དང་།
།སངས་རྒྱས་སྲས་ཀྱིས་རབ་ཏུ་གང་བར་ཤོག

chok chou galé zhing nam ji nyé pa
dédak gyachér yongsou dakpar gyour
jangchoub shing wang droung shék gyalwa tang
sangyé sékyi rabtou gangwar sho

།ཕྱོགས་བཅུའི་སེམས་ཅན་གང་རྣམས་ཇི་སྙེད་པ།
།དེ་དག་རྟག་ཏུ་ནད་མེད་བདེ་བར་གྱུར།
།འགྲོ་བ་ཀུན་གྱི་ཆོས་ཀྱི་དོན་རྣམས་ནི།
།མཐུན་པར་གྱུར་ཅིང་རེ་བ་འང་འགྲུབ་པར་ཤོག

chok chou'i semchen gang nam ji nyépa
dédak taktou némé déwar gyour
drowa küngyi chökyi dön nam ni
tünpar gyour ching réwa'ang droub par sho

May the buddhas of the past and those dwelling presently
In the worlds of the ten directions be honored by offerings.
May those yet to come swiftly fulfill their aspiration
And attain buddhahood through the stages of awakening.

Wherever there are world systems in the ten directions
May they, in their great number, become perfectly pure.
May these universes abound in victorious ones
Who have come before the tree of enlightenment,
Accompanied by bodhisattvas, their spiritual heirs.

May each and every one of the manifold beings
Of the ten directions always be happy and healthy.
May all beings find true purpose in the Dharma,
And in harmony with this, may their hopes be fulfilled.

།བྱང་ཆུབ་སྤྱོད་པ་དག་ནི་བདག་སྤྱོད་ཅིང་།
།འགྲོ་བ་ཀུན་ཏུ་སྐྱེ་བ་དྲན་པར་གྱུར།
།ཚེ་རབས་ཀུན་ཏུ་འཆི་འཕོ་སྐྱེ་བ་ན།
།རྟག་ཏུ་བདག་ནི་རབ་ཏུ་འབྱུང་བར་ཤོག

jangchoub chöpa dakni da chö ching
drowa küntou kyéwa drenpar gyour
tsérab küntou chipo kyéwa na
taktou dani rabtou joungwar sho

།རྒྱལ་བ་ཀུན་གྱི་རྗེས་སུ་སློབ་གྱུར་ཏེ།
།བཟང་པོ་སྤྱོད་པ་ཡོངས་སུ་རྫོགས་བྱེད་ཅིང་།
།ཚུལ་ཁྲིམས་སྤྱོད་པ་དྲི་མེད་ཡོངས་དག་པར།
།རྟག་ཏུ་མ་ཉམས་སྐྱོན་མེད་སྤྱོད་པར་ཤོག

gyalwa kün gyi jésou lob gyour té
zangpo chöpa yongsou dzok jé ching
tsültrim chöpa drimé yong dakpar
taktou ma nyam kyönmé chöpar sho

།ལྷ་ཡི་སྐད་དང་ཀླུ་དང་གནོད་སྦྱིན་སྐད།
།གྲུལ་བུམ་དག་དང་མི་ཡི་སྐད་རྣམས་དང་།
།འགྲོ་བ་ཀུན་གྱི་སྒྲ་སྐད་ཇི་ཙམ་པར།
།ཐམས་ཅད་སྐད་དུ་བདག་གིས་ཆོས་བསྟན་ཏོ།

lhayi ké tang lou tang nöjin ké
droulboum dak tang miyi ké nam tang
drowa kün gyi dra ké ji tsampar
tamché kédou dagi chö ten to

May I carry out the many forms of enlightened conduct,
And remember past lives when experiencing each new one.
During each successive death, transmigration, and rebirth,
May I always embrace religious life, and renounce.

Following the example of the victorious ones,
May I fully accomplish excellent conduct,
And may my moral behavior be flawless and pure.
May I conduct myself faultlessly in all situations.

May I communicate the Buddhadharma
In every language known to sentient beings,
The tongues of gods, nāgas, djinns, trolls,
And all languages spoken by humankind.

།དེས་ཞིང་ཕ་རོལ་ཕྱིན་ལ་རབ་བརྩོན་ཏེ།
།བྱང་ཆུབ་སེམས་ནི་ནམ་ཡང་བརྗེད་མ་གྱུར།
།སྡིག་པ་གང་རྣམས་སྒྲིབ་པར་འགྱུར་བ་དག
།དེ་དག་མ་ལུས་ཡོངས་སུ་བྱང་བར་ཤོག

déshing paröl jin la rab tsön té
jangchoub semni namyang jé ma gyour
dikpa gang nam dribpar gyourwa dak
dédak malü yongsou jangwar sho

།ལས་དང་ཉོན་མོངས་བདུད་ཀྱི་ལས་རྣམས་ལས།
།གྲོལ་ཞིང་འཇིག་རྟེན་འགྲོ་བ་རྣམས་སུ་ཡང་།
།ཇི་ལྟར་པདྨོ་ཆུས་མི་ཆགས་པ་བཞིན།
།ཉི་ཟླ་ནམ་མཁར་ཐོགས་པ་མེད་ལྟར་སྤྱད།

lé tang nyönmong dükyi lé nam lé
dröl zhing jikten drowa namsou yang
jitar pémo chü mi chakpa zhin
nyida namkhar tokpa mé tar ché

།ཞིང་གི་ཁྱོན་དང་ཕྱོགས་རྣམས་ཇི་ཙམ་པར།
།ངན་སོང་སྡུག་བསྔལ་རབ་ཏུ་ཞི་བར་བྱེད།
།བདེ་བ་དག་ལ་འགྲོ་བ་ཀུན་འགོད་ཅིང་།
།འགྲོ་བ་ཐམས་ཅད་ལ་ནི་ཕན་པར་སྤྱད།

zhingi khyön tang chok nam ji tsam par
ngen song douk ngal rabtou zhiwar jé
déwa dakla drowa kün gö ching
drowa tamché lani penpar ché

Gentle and wise, may I apply myself
To the transcendent qualities of the pāramitās,
While never losing sight of awakening mind.
As for all harmful acts that have resulted in veils,
May they be entirely purified, without exception.

May I be liberated from negative karma,
Disturbing emotions, and the actions of māras.
Wherever there are world systems and beings,
May I be like the lotus, not clung to by water,
And the sun and the moon, unhindered in the sky.

Throughout each of the realms and in every direction,
May I pacify all suffering of the unfortunate realms.
May I establish all beings in happiness,
And may I be of assistance to every one.

།བྱང་ཆུབ་སྤྱོད་པ་ཡོངས་སུ་རྫོགས་བྱེད་ཅིང་།
།སེམས་ཅན་ཅན་དག་གི་སྤྱོད་དང་མཐུན་པར་འཇུག
།བཟང་པོ་སྤྱོད་པ་དག་ནི་རབ་སྟོན་ཅིང་།
།མ་འོངས་བསྐལ་པ་ཀུན་ཏུ་སྤྱོད་པར་གྱུར།

jangchoub chöpa yongsou dzok jé ching
semchen dakgi chötang tünpar jouk
zangpo chöpa dakni rab tön ching
ma'ong kalpa küntou chöpar gyour

།བདག་གི་སྤྱོད་དང་མཚུངས་པར་གང་སྤྱོད་པ།
།དེ་དག་དང་ནི་རྟག་ཏུ་འགྲོགས་པར་ཤོག
།ལུས་དང་ངག་རྣམས་དང་ནི་སེམས་ཀྱིས་ཀྱང་།
།སྤྱོད་པ་དག་དང་སྨོན་ལམ་གཅིག་ཏུ་སྤྱད།

dagi chö tang tsoungpar gang chöpa
dédak tangni taktou drokpar sho
lütang ngak nam tang ni semkyi kyang
chöpa dak tang mönlam chik tu ché

།བདག་ལ་ཕན་པར་འདོད་པའི་གྲོགས་པོ་དག
།བཟང་པོའི་སྤྱོད་པ་རབ་ཏུ་སྟོན་པ་རྣམས།
།དེ་དག་དང་ཡང་རྟག་ཏུ་ཕྲད་པར་ཤོག
།དེ་དག་བདག་གིས་ནམ་ཡང་ཡིད་མི་འབྱུང་།

dala penpar döpé drokpo dak
zangpo'i chöpa rabtou tönpa nam
dédak tang yang taktou trépar sho
dédak dagi namyang yi mi young

96

May I perfect the practice of enlightened conduct
In accord with the various lifestyles of beings.
May I fully exemplify excellent conduct,
And continue to do so during all future eons.

May I always be accompanied by those friends
Whose practice and conduct resemble my own.
With regard to our body, speech, and mind,
May all of our actions and prayers be as one.

May I always encounter companions
Who exemplify excellent conduct
And have my well-being at heart.
May I never let these teachers down.

།སངས་རྒྱས་སྲས་ཀྱིས་བསྐོར་བའི་མགོན་པོ་རྣམས།
།མངོན་སུམ་རྟག་ཏུ་བདག་གིས་རྒྱལ་བ་བལྟ།
།མ་འོངས་བསྐལ་པ་ཀུན་ཏུ་མི་སྐྱོ་བར།
།དེ་དག་ལ་ཡང་མཆོད་པ་རྒྱ་ཆེར་བགྱི།

sangyé sékyi korwé gönpo nam
ngönsoum taktou dagi gyalwa ta
ma'ong kalpa küntou mi kyowar
dédak la yang chöpa gyachér gyi

།རྒྱལ་བ་རྣམས་ཀྱི་དམ་པའི་ཆོས་འཛིན་ཅིང་།
།བྱང་ཆུབ་སྤྱོད་པ་ཀུན་ཏུ་སྣང་བར་བྱེད།
།བཟང་པོ་སྤྱོད་པ་རྣམ་པར་སྦྱང་བ་ཡང་།
།མ་འོངས་བསྐལ་པ་ཀུན་ཏུ་སྤྱད་པར་བགྱི།

gyalwa namkyi dampé chö dzin ching
jangchoub chöpa küntou nangwar jé
zangpo chöpa nampar jangwa yang
ma'ong kalpa küntou chépar gyi

།སྲིད་པ་ཐམས་ཅད་དུ་ཡང་འཁོར་བ་ན།
།བསོད་ནམས་ཡེ་ཤེས་དག་ནི་མི་ཟད་སྙེད།
།ཐབས་དང་ཤེས་རབ་ཏིང་འཛིན་རྣམ་ཐར་དང་།
།ཡོན་ཏན་ཀུན་གྱི་མི་ཟད་མཛོད་དུ་གྱུར།

sipa tamché douyang khorwa na
sönam yéshé dakni mizé nyé
tab tang shérab ting dzin namtar tang
yönten küngyi mizé dzö dougyour

May I always directly perceive the victorious ones:
The protectors and their entourage of bodhisattvas.
Throughout all future eons, may I never grow weary
Of honoring them with remarkably vast offerings.

May I uphold the genuine Dharma of the buddhas,
And make enlightened conduct fully manifest.
May I be perfectly trained in excellent conduct,
Wholeheartedly continuing for eons to come.

Through all my existences, be they within saṃsāra,
May I acquire inexhaustible merit and wisdom.
May these become a never-ending treasure of qualities:
Methods, superior knowledge, samādhi, and liberation.

།རྡུལ་གཅིག་སྟེང་ན་རྡུལ་སྙེད་ཞིང་རྣམས་ཏེ།
།ཞིང་དེར་བསམ་གྱིས་མི་ཁྱབ་སངས་རྒྱས་རྣམས།
།སངས་རྒྱས་སྲས་ཀྱི་དབུས་ན་བཞུགས་པ་ལ།
།བྱང་ཆུབ་སྤྱོད་པ་སྤྱོད་ཅིང་བལྟ་བར་བགྱི།

dül chik teng na dül nyé zhing nam té
zhing dér samgyi mi khyab sangyé nam
sangyé sékyi üna zhouk pa la
jangchoub chöpa chö ching tawar gyi

།དེ་ལྟར་མ་ལུས་ཐམས་ཅད་ཕྱོགས་སུ་ཡང་།
།སྐྲ་ཙམ་ཁྱོན་ལ་དུས་གསུམ་ཚད་སྙེད་ཀྱི།
།སངས་རྒྱས་རྒྱ་མཚོ་ཞིང་རྣམས་རྒྱ་མཚོ་དང་།
།བསྐལ་པ་རྒྱ་མཚོར་སྤྱོད་ཅིང་རབ་ཏུ་འཇུག

détar malü tamché chok sou yang
tra tsam khyön la düsoum tsé nyé kyi
sangyé gyatso zhing nam gyatso tang
kalpa gyatsor chöching rabtou jouk

།གསུང་གཅིག་ཡན་ལག་རྒྱ་མཚོའི་སྒྲ་སྐད་ཀྱིས།
།རྒྱལ་བ་ཀུན་དབྱངས་ཡན་ལག་རྣམ་དག་པ།
།འགྲོ་བ་ཀུན་གྱི་བསམ་པ་ཇི་བཞིན་དབྱངས།
།སངས་རྒྱས་གསུང་ལ་རྟག་ཏུ་འཇུག་པར་བགྱི།

soung chik yenlak gyatso'i draké kyi
gyalwa kün yang yenlak namdak pa
drowa kün gyi sampa ji zhin yang
sangyé soung la taktou jouk par gyi

Atop one particle, there are as many realms as atoms;
In each pure realm, more buddhas than can be imagined
Reside amidst bodhisattvas, their spiritual heirs.
May I see them and emulate their enlightened activity.

Likewise, in absolutely every direction,
Within the space on the tip of one hair,
There are oceans of buddhas of past, present, and future,
Oceans of pure realms and oceans of eons.
May I fully take part in this enlightened activity.

The sound of one instance of the Buddha's speech,
With its ocean of qualities, holds the pure range
Of harmonious expressions of all victorious ones;
It is the very melody of each being's understanding.
May I always engage in the speech of the buddhas.

།དུས་གསུམ་གཤེགས་པ་རྒྱལ་བ་ཐམས་ཅད་དག
།འཁོར་ལོའི་ཚུལ་རྣམས་རབ་ཏུ་བསྐོར་བ་ཡིས།
།དེ་དག་གི་ཡང་གསུང་དབྱངས་མི་ཟད་ལ།
།བློ་ཡི་སྟོབས་ཀྱིས་བདག་ཀྱང་རབ་ཏུ་འཇུག

düsoum shékpé gyalwa tamché dak
khorlo'i tsülnam rabtou korwa yi
dédak gi yang soung yang mizé la
lo yi tob kyi dakyang rabtou jouk

།མ་འོངས་བསྐལ་པ་ཐམས་ཅད་འཇུག་པར་ཡང་།
།སྐད་ཅིག་གཅིག་གིས་བདག་ཀྱང་འཇུག་པར་བགྱི།
།གང་ཡང་བསྐལ་པ་དུས་གསུམ་ཚད་དེ་དག
།སྐད་ཅིག་ཆ་ཤས་ཀྱིས་ནི་ཞུགས་པར་བྱ།

ma'ong kalpa tamché joukpar yang
kéchik chiki dakyang jouk par gyi
gang yang kalpa düsoum tsé dédak
kéchik chashé kyi ni zhouk par ché

།དུས་གསུམ་གཤེགས་པ་མི་ཡི་སེང་གི་གང་།
།དེ་དག་སྐད་ཅིག་གཅིག་ལ་བདག་གིས་བལྟ།
།རྟག་ཏུ་དེ་དག་གི་ནི་སྤྱོད་ཡུལ་ལ།
།སྒྱུ་མར་གྱུར་པའི་རྣམ་ཐར་སྟོབས་ཀྱིས་འཇུག

düsoum shékpa miyi séngé gang
dédak kéchik chik la dagi ta
taktou dédak gi ni chöyoul la
gyoumar gyourpé namtar tobkyi jouk

All victorious ones of past, present, and future
Fully turn the wheel of Dharma in a variety of ways.
Through the power of mind, may I also participate
In the boundless expression of their melodious speech.

In a single instant, may I engage in
All future eons which will be experienced.
In just a split second, may I take part in
Any and all of the eons of the three times.

In the space of a single moment, may I behold
All lions among men of past, present, and future.
May I continually engage in their field of experience
Through the power of illusion-like spiritual liberation.

།གང་ཡང་དུས་གསུམ་དག་གི་ཞིང་བཀོད་པ།
།དེ་དག་རྫུལ་གཅིག་སྟེང་དུ་མངོན་པར་བསྒྲུབ།
།དེ་ལྟར་མ་ལུས་ཕྱོགས་རྣམས་ཐམས་ཅད་དུ།
།རྒྱལ་བ་རྣམས་ཀྱི་ཞིང་གི་བཀོད་ལ་འཇུག

gangyang düsoum dakgi zhing köpa
dédak dülchik téngdou ngönpar droup
détar malü choknam tamché dou
gyalwa namkyi zhingi köla jouk

།གང་ཡང་མ་བྱོན་འཇིག་རྟེན་སྒྲོན་མ་རྣམས།
།དེ་དག་རིམ་པར་འཚང་རྒྱ་འཁོར་ལོ་སྐོར།
།མྱ་ངན་འདས་པ་རབ་ཏུ་ཞི་མཐའ་སྟོན།
།མགོན་པོ་ཀུན་གྱི་དྲུང་དུ་བདག་མཆིའོ༔

gangyang ma jön jikten drönma nam
dédak rimpar tsang gya khorlo kor
nya ngen dépa rabtou zhita tön
gönpo küngyi droungdou dachi-o

The clusters of galaxies of past, present, and future
Have all been established atop a single particle.
Accordingly, in all directions, without exception,
May I take part in the pure realms of the victors.

The lanterns of the world who have yet to come
Will all, by stages, become fully enlightened,
Turn the wheel of the Dharma, and demonstrate
The state beyond suffering, ultimate peace.
May I be in the presence of all those protectors.

།ཀུན་ནས་མྱུར་བའི་རྫུ་འཕྲུལ་སྟོབས་རྣམས་དང་།
།ཀུན་ནས་སྒོ་ཡི་ཐེག་པའི་སྟོབས་དག་དང་།
།ཀུན་ཏུ་ཡོན་ཏན་སྤྱོད་པའི་སྟོབས་རྣམས་དང་།
།ཀུན་ཏུ་ཁྱབ་པ་བྱམས་པ་དག་གི་སྟོབས།
།ཀུན་ཏུ་དགེ་བའི་བསོད་ནམས་སྟོབས་རྣམས་དང་།
།ཆགས་པ་མེད་པར་གྱུར་པའི་ཡེ་ཤེས་སྟོབས།
།ཤེས་རབ་ཐབས་དང་ཏིང་འཛིན་སྟོབས་དག་གིས།
།བྱང་ཆུབ་སྟོབས་རྣམས་ཡང་དག་སྒྲུབ་པར་བྱེད།

künné nyourwé dzoutrül tob nam tang
künné goyi tékpé tob dak tang
küntou yönten chöpé tob nam tang
küntou khyabpa jampa dak gi tob
küntou géwé sönam tob nam tang
chakpa mépar gyourwé yéshé tob
shérab tab tang ting dzin tob dak gi
jangchoub tob nam yangdak droubpar jé

།ལས་ཀྱི་སྟོབས་རྣམས་ཡོངས་སུ་དག་བྱེད་ཅིང་།
།ཉོན་མོངས་སྟོབས་རྣམས་ཀུན་ཏུ་འཇོམས་པར་བྱེད།
།བདུད་ཀྱི་སྟོབས་རྣམས་སྟོབས་མེད་རབ་བྱེད་ཅིང་།
།བཟང་པོ་སྤྱོད་པའི་སྟོབས་ནི་རྫོགས་པར་བགྱི།

lékyi tobnam yongsou dak jé ching
nyönmong tob nam küntou jompar jé
dükyi tob nam tob mé rab jé ching
zangpo chöpé tobni dzokpar gyi

106

By virtue of the powers of miraculous swiftness,
The powers of the manifold approaches of the yānas,
The powers of practice endowed with all qualities,
The powers of omnipresent lovingkindness,
The powers of perfectly virtuous goodness,
The powers of unbounded timeless wisdom,
The powers of knowledge, means, and deep meditation,
May I truly achieve the many powers of awakening.

May I completely purify the powers of karma,
Fully defeat the powers of the afflictions,
Utterly disable the powers of the māras,
And bring the power of excellent conduct to perfection.

།ཞིང་རྣམས་རྒྱ་མཚོ་རྣམ་པར་དག་བྱེད་ཅིང་།
།སེམས་ཅན་རྒྱ་མཚོ་དག་ནི་རྣམ་པར་འགྲོལ།
།ཆོས་རྣམས་རྒྱ་མཚོ་རབ་ཏུ་མཐོང་བྱེད་ཅིང་།
།ཡེ་ཤེས་རྒྱ་མཚོ་རབ་ཏུ་གོམས་པར་བྱེད།
།སྤྱོད་པ་རྒྱ་མཚོ་རྣམ་པར་དག་བྱེད་ཅིང་།
།སྨོན་ལམ་རྒྱ་མཚོ་རབ་ཏུ་རྫོགས་པར་བྱེད།
།སངས་རྒྱས་རྒྱ་མཚོ་རབ་ཏུ་མཆོད་བྱེད་ཅིང་།
།བསྐལ་པ་རྒྱ་མཚོར་མི་སྐྱོ་སྤྱོད་པར་བགྱི།

zhingnam gyatso nampar dak jé ching
semchen gyatso dakni nampar dröl
chönam gyatso rabtou tong jé ching
yéshé gyatso rabtou gompar jé
chöpa gyatso nampar dak jé ching
mönlam gyatso rabtou dzokpar jé
sangyé gyatso rabtou chö jé ching
kalpa gyatsor mikyo chépar gyi

།གང་ཡང་དུས་གསུམ་གཤེགས་པའི་རྒྱལ་བ་ཡི།
།བྱང་ཆུབ་སྤྱོད་པའི་སྨོན་ལམ་བྱེ་བྲག་རྣམས།
།བཟང་པོ་སྤྱོད་པས་བྱང་ཆུབ་སངས་རྒྱས་ནས།
།དེ་ཀུན་བདག་གིས་མ་ལུས་རྫོགས་པར་བགྱི།

gangyang düsoum shékpé gyalwa yi
jangchoub chöpé mönlam jédrak nam
zangpo chöpé jangchoub sangyé né
dé kün dagi malü dzok par gyi

May I totally purify oceans of realms,
Entirely liberate oceans of beings,
Clearly behold oceans of Dharma,
Wholly integrate oceans of wisdom,
Patently clarify oceans of conduct,
Perfectly fulfill oceans of aspirations,
Honor oceans of buddhas with my offerings,
And practice tirelessly during oceans of eons.

Once I have awakened and attained buddhahood
By means of the practice of excellent conduct,
May I fulfill all special wishes of enlightened conduct
Expressed by victorious ones of past, present and future.

།རྒྱལ་བ་ཀུན་གྱི་སྲས་ཀྱི་ཐུ་བོ་པ།
།གང་གི་མིང་ནི་ཀུན་ཏུ་བཟང་ཞེས་བྱ།
།མཁས་པ་དེ་དང་མཚུངས་པར་སྤྱོད་པའི་ཕྱིར།
།དགེ་བ་འདི་དག་ཐམས་ཅད་རབ་ཏུ་བསྔོ།

gyalwa küngyi sékyi toubo pa
gangi ming ni küntou zang zhé ja
khépa dé tang tsoungpar chépé chir
géwa didak tamché rabtou ngo

།ལུས་དང་ངག་དང་ཡིད་ཀྱང་རྣམ་དག་ཅིང་།
།སྤྱོད་པ་རྣམ་དག་ཞིང་རྣམས་ཡོངས་དག་དང་།
།བསྔོ་བའང་བཟང་པོ་མཁས་པ་ཅི་འདྲ་བ།
།དེ་འདྲར་བདག་ཀྱང་དེ་དང་མཚུངས་པར་ཤོག

lü tang ngak tang yi kyang namdak ching
chöpa namdak zhingnam yongdak tang
ngowa'ang zangpo khépa chi drawa
dédrar dakyang détang tsoung par sho

།ཀུན་ནས་དགེ་བ་བཟང་པོ་སྤྱོད་པའི་ཕྱིར།
།འཇམ་དཔལ་གྱི་ནི་སྨོན་ལམ་སྤྱོད་པར་བགྱི།
།མ་འོངས་བསྐལ་པ་ཀུན་ཏུ་མི་སྐྱོ་བར།
།དེ་ཡི་བྱ་བ་མ་ལུས་རྫོགས་པར་བགྱི།

künné géwa zangpo chöpé chir
jampel gyini mönlam chépar gyi
ma'ong kalpa küntou mi kyowar
déyi jawa malü dzokpar gyi

The eldest son of the victorious ones
Is known as Samantabhadra, the All-Excellent.
In order to equal his masterful skill,
I perfectly dedicate all forms of merit.

May I be comparable to Samantabhadra:
His utterly pure body, speech, and mind,
His totally pure conduct, perfectly pure realms,
And superior skill in dedicating merit.

So as to completely achieve excellent goodness,
I will carry out Mañjuśrī's aspiration prayers.
Continuing tirelessly throughout future eons,
I will accomplish every last one of his activities.

།སྤྱོད་པ་དག་ནི་ཚད་ཡོད་མ་གྱུར་ཅིག
།ཡོན་ཏན་རྣམས་ཀྱང་ཚད་གཟུང་མེད་པར་ཤོག
།སྤྱོད་པ་ཚད་མེད་པ་ལ་གནས་ནས་ཀྱང་།
།དེ་དག་འཕྲུལ་པ་ཐམས་ཅད་འཚལ་བར་བགྱི།

chöpa dakni tséyö magyour chik
yönten nam kyang tsézoung mépar sho
chöpa tsémé pa la né né kyang
dédak trülpa tamché tsalwar gyi

།ནམ་མཁའི་མཐའ་ཕྱུག་གྱུར་པ་ཇི་ཙམ་པར།
།སེམས་ཅན་མ་ལུས་མཐའ་ཡས་དེ་བཞིན་ཏེ།
།ཇི་ཙམ་ལས་དང་ཉོན་མོངས་མཐར་གྱུར་པ།
།བདག་གི་སྨོན་ལམ་མཐའ་ཡང་དེ་ཙམ་མོ།

namkhé tartouk gyourpa ji tsampar
semchen malü tayang dé zhin té
ji tsam lé tang nyönmong tar gyour pa
dagi mönlam tayang dé tsammo

May my actions be free of limitations,
And my qualities also be without bounds.
May I remain engaged in activities beyond measure,
And may I come to know all of their manifestations.

There are countless beings, as limitless
As the very confines of the endless sky.
Whatever their karma and afflictions may be,
May my wishing prayers encompass them all.

།གང་ཡང་ཕྱོགས་བཅུའི་ཞིང་རྣམས་མཐའ་ཡས་པ།
།རིན་ཆེན་བརྒྱན་ཏེ་རྒྱལ་བ་རྣམས་ལ་ཕུལ།
།ལྷ་དང་མི་ཡི་བདེ་བའི་མཆོག་རྣམས་ཀྱང་།
།ཞིང་གི་རྡུལ་སྙེད་བསྐལ་པར་ཕུལ་བ་བས།
།གང་གིས་བསྟོ་བའི་རྒྱལ་པོ་འདི་ཐོས་ནས།
།བྱང་ཆུབ་མཆོག་གི་རྗེས་སུ་རབ་མོས་ཤིང་།
།ལན་ཅིག་ཙམ་ཡང་དད་པ་སྐྱེད་པ་ནི།
།བསོད་ནམས་དམ་པའི་མཆོག་ཏུ་འདི་འགྱུར་རོ།

gangyang chokchou'i zhingnam tayé pa
rinchen gyen té gyalwa nam la pül
lha tang miyi déwé chok nam kyang
zhingi dül nyé kalpar pülwa wé
gangi ngowé gyalpo di tö né
jangchoub chokgi jésou rab mö shing
len chik tsam yang dépa kyépa ni
sönam dampé choktou di gyour ro

།གང་གིས་བཟང་སྤྱོད་སྨོན་ལམ་འདི་བཏབ་པས།
།དེས་ནི་ངན་སོང་ཐམས་ཅད་སྤངས་པར་འགྱུར།
།དེས་ནི་གྲོགས་པོ་ངན་པ་སྤངས་པ་ཡིན།
།སྣང་བ་མཐའ་ཡས་དེ་ཡང་དེས་མྱུར་མཐོང་།

gangi zangchö mönlam di tab pé
déni ngen song tamché pangpar gyour
déni drokpo ngenpa pangpa yin
nangwa tayé déyang dé nyour tong

We may embellish the infinite realms of the ten directions
With precious gems and present them to the victorious ones;
We may offer the finest pleasures of gods and humans
During as many eons as there are atoms in the universe.
Even so, paramount indeed is the exceptional merit
Of those of us who have heard this King of Dedications,
Are truly determined to pursue supreme enlightenment,
And give rise to genuine faith, be it just for a moment.

Those who practice this Prayer of Excellent Conduct
Will turn away from rebirth in the lower realms,
Sever all ties to unwholesome companions,
And promptly behold Amitābha, Infinite Light.

།དེ་དག་སྙེད་པ་རབ་སྙེད་བདེ་བར་འཚོ།
།མི་ཚེ་འདིར་ཡང་དེ་དག་ལེགས་པར་འོང་།
།ཀུན་ཏུ་བཟང་པོ་དེ་ཡང་ཅི་འདྲ་བར།
།དེ་དག་རིང་པོར་མི་ཐོགས་དེ་བཞིན་འགྱུར།

dédak nyépa rab nyé déwar tso
mitsé diryang dédak lékpar ong
küntou zangpo déyang chi drawar
dédak ringpor mitok dézhin gyour

།མཚམས་མེད་ལྔ་པོ་དག་གི་སྡིག་པ་རྣམས།
།གང་གིས་མི་ཤེས་དབང་གིས་བྱས་པ་དག
།དེ་ཡིས་བཟང་པོ་སྤྱོད་པ་འདི་བརྗོད་ན།
།མྱུར་དུ་མ་ལུས་ཡོངས་སུ་བྱང་བར་འགྱུར།

tsammé ngapo dagi dikpa nam
gangi mishé wangi jépa dak
déyi zangpo chöpa di jö na
nyourdou malü yongsou jangwar gyour

།ཡེ་ཤེས་དང་ནི་གཟུགས་དང་མཚན་རྣམས་དང་།
།རིགས་དང་ཁ་དོག་རྣམས་དང་ལྡན་པར་འགྱུར།
།བདུད་དང་མུ་སྟེགས་མང་པོས་དེ་མི་ཐུབ།
།འཇིག་རྟེན་གསུམ་པོ་ཀུན་ནའང་མཆོད་པར་འགྱུར།

yéshé tang ni zouk tang tsen nam tang
rik tang khadok nam tang denpar gyour
dü tang mouték mangpö dé mi toub
jikten soumpo kün na'ang chöpar gyour

They will be perfectly comfortable and lead happy lives;
In this lifetime as well, comfort and happiness will reign.
Without delay, they will become similar in every way
To Samantabhadra, the All-Excellent One.

If this Prayer of Excellent Conduct is recited
By those who have committed, by reason of ignorance,
The five most negative acts of direct consequence,
These all will be quickly and thoroughly purified.

Practitioners will have wisdom, the shapeliest physique,
Excellent signs, a noble family, and a fine complexion.
The many māras and heretics will be powerless against them,
And they will be honored throughout the three worlds.

།བྱང་ཆུབ་ཤིང་དབང་དྲུང་དུ་དེ་མྱུར་འགྲོ །
།སོང་ནས་སེམས་ཅན་ཕན་ཕྱིར་དེར་འདུག་སྟེ །
།བྱང་ཆུབ་སངས་རྒྱས་འཁོར་ལོ་རབ་ཏུ་སྐོར །
།བདུད་རྣམས་སྡེ་དང་བཅས་པ་ཐམས་ཅད་བཏུལ །

jangchoub shingwang droungdou dé nyour dro
song né semchen penchir dér douk té
jangchoub sangyé khorlo rabtou kor
dünam dé tang chépa tamché tül

།གང་ཡང་བཟང་པོ་སྤྱོད་པའི་སྨོན་ལམ་འདི །
།འཆང་བ་དང་ནི་སྟོན་ཏམ་ཀློག་པ་ཡི །
།དེ་ཡི་རྣམ་པར་སྨིན་པ་སངས་རྒྱས་མཁྱེན །
།བྱང་ཆུབ་མཆོག་ལ་སོམ་ཉི་མ་བྱེད་ཅིག །

gangyang zangpo chöpé mönlam di
changwa tang ni töntam lokpa yi
déyi nampar minpa sangyé khyen
jangchoub chokla som nyi ma jé chik

།འཇམ་དཔལ་ཇི་ལྟར་མཁྱེན་ཅིང་དཔའ་བ་དང་ །
།ཀུན་ཏུ་བཟང་པོ་དེ་ཡང་དེ་བཞིན་ཏེ །
།དེ་དག་ཀུན་གྱི་རྗེས་སུ་བདག་སློབ་ཅིང་ །
།དགེ་བ་འདི་དག་ཐམས་ཅད་རབ་ཏུ་བསྔོ །

jampel jitar khyen ching pawa tang
küntou zangpo déyang dézhin té
dédak küngyi jésou dalob ching
géwa didak tamché rab tou ngo

They will go quickly before the great bodhi tree,
And settle there for the benefit of sentient beings.
As awakened buddhas they will turn the wheel of Dharma,
Prevailing against all of the māras and their legions.

The buddhas alone fathom the full karmic fruition
For those who take this Prayer of Excellent Activity
To heart by expounding it, or reading and reciting it.
Have no doubt: the outcome is supreme awakening!

May I train by emulating the examples of Mañjuśrī,
With his momentous knowledge and great courage,
And Samantabhadra, whose qualities are identical;
Like them, I perfectly dedicate all forms of merit.

།དུས་གསུམ་གཤེགས་པ་རྒྱལ་བ་ཐམས་ཅད་ཀྱིས། །
།བསྔོ་བ་གང་ལ་མཆོག་ཏུ་བསྔགས་པ་དེས། །
།བདག་གི་དགེ་བའི་རྩ་བ་འདི་ཀུན་ཀྱང་། །
།བཟང་པོ་སྤྱོད་ཕྱིར་རབ་ཏུ་བསྔོ་བར་བགྱི། །

düsoum shékpé gyalwa tamché kyi
ngowa gang la chok tou ngakpa dé
dagi géwé tsawa di kün kyang
zangpo chö chir rabtou ngowar gyi

།བདག་ནི་འཆི་བའི་དུས་བྱེད་གྱུར་པ་ན། །
།སྒྲིབ་པ་ཐམས་ཅད་དག་ནི་ཕྱིར་བསལ་ཏེ། །
།མངོན་སུམ་སྣང་བ་མཐའ་ཡས་དེ་མཐོང་ནས། །
།བདེ་བ་ཅན་གྱི་ཞིང་དེར་རབ་ཏུ་འགྲོ། །

dani chiwé düjé gyourpa na
dribpa tamché dakni chir sal té
ngön soum nangwa tayé dé tong né
déwachen gyi zhing dér rabtou dro

།དེར་སོང་ནས་ནི་སྨོན་ལམ་འདི་དག་ཀྱང་། །
།ཐམས་ཅད་མ་ལུས་མངོན་དུ་འགྱུར་བར་ཤོག །
།དེ་དག་མ་ལུས་བདག་གིས་ཡོངས་སུ་བཀང་། །
།འཇིག་རྟེན་ཇི་སྲིད་སེམས་ཅན་ཕན་པར་བགྱི། །

dér song né ni mönlam didak kyang
tamché malü ngöndou gyourwar sho
dédak malü dagi yongsou kang
jikten jisi semchen penpar gyi

For the sake of the practice of excellent conduct,
I completely dedicate all of my roots of goodness
By means of those dedications praised as supreme
By the victorious ones of past, present, and future.

When the time has come for me to die,
And all of my veils, now purified, disappear,
May I directly behold Amitābha, Infinite Light,
And proceed with certainty to the realm of joy.

Once there, may these and all other prayers,
Without a single exception, become manifest.
May I perfectly fulfill each and every one,
Helping beings for as long as the universe exists.

།རྒྱལ་བའི་དཀྱིལ་འཁོར་བཟང་ཞིང་དགའ་བ་དེར།
།པདྨོ་དམ་པ་ཤིན་ཏུ་མཛེས་ལས་སྐྱེས།
།སྣང་བ་མཐའ་ཡས་རྒྱལ་བས་མངོན་སུམ་དུ།
།ལུང་བསྟན་པ་ཡང་བདག་གིས་དེར་ཐོབ་ཤོག

gyalwé kyilkhor zang zhing gawa dér
pémo dampa zhintou dzé lé kyé
nangwa tayé gyalwé ngön soum dou
loung tenpa yang dagi dér tob sho

།དེར་ནི་བདག་གིས་ལུང་བསྟན་རབ་ཐོབ་ནས།
།སྤྲུལ་པ་མང་པོ་བྱེ་བ་ཕྲག་བརྒྱ་ཡིས།
།བློ་ཡི་སྟོབས་ཀྱིས་ཕྱོགས་བཅུ་རྣམས་སུ་ཡང་།
།སེམས་ཅན་རྣམས་ལ་ཕན་པ་མང་པོ་བགྱི།

dérni dagi loungten rab tob né
trülpa mangpo jéwa trak gya yi
loyi tob kyi chok chou nam sou yang
semchen namla penpa mangpo gyi

།བཟང་པོ་སྤྱོད་པའི་སྨོན་ལམ་བཏབ་པ་ཡི།
།དགེ་བ་ཅུང་ཟད་བདག་གིས་ཅི་བསགས་པ།
།དེས་ནི་འགྲོ་བའི་སྨོན་ལམ་དགེ་བ་རྣམས།
།སྐད་ཅིག་གཅིག་གིས་ཐམས་ཅད་འབྱོར་བར་ཤོག

zangpo chöpé mönlam tabpa yi
géwa choungzé dagi chi sak pa
déni drowé mönlam géwa nam
kéchik chikgi tamché jorwar sho

122

May I be reborn in a supremely beautiful lotus
In the excellent, joyous mandala of the buddhas.
There, may I obtain my prophetic revelation
Directly from Amitābha, the Victorious One.

Once the prophecy has been fully achieved,
May I serve the beings of the ten directions
In a number of ways through the power of mind
Of many hundreds times millions of emanations.

By whatever small merit I may have garnered
By practicing this Prayer of Excellent Activity,
May the meritorious aspirations of sentient beings
All be accomplished in the space of one instant.

།བཟང་པོ་སྤྱོད་པ་ཡོངས་སུ་བསྐྱོས་པ་ལས།
།བསོད་ནམས་མཐའ་ཡས་དམ་པ་གང་ཐོབ་དེས།
།འགྲོ་བ་སྡུག་བསྔལ་ཆུ་བོར་བྱིང་བ་རྣམས།
།འོད་དཔག་མེད་པའི་གནས་རབ་ཐོབ་པར་ཤོག

zangpo chöpa yongsou ngöpa lé
sönam tayé dampa gang tob dé
drowa douk ngal choubor jingwa nam
öpa mépé nérab tob par cho

།སྨོན་ལམ་རྒྱལ་པོ་འདི་དག་མཆོག་གི་གཙོ།
།མཐའ་ཡས་འགྲོ་བ་ཀུན་ལ་ཕན་བྱེད་ཅིང་།
།ཀུན་ཏུ་བཟང་པོས་བརྒྱན་པའི་གཞུང་གྲུབ་སྟེ།
།ངན་སོང་གནས་རྣམས་མ་ལུས་སྟོངས་པར་ཤོག།

mönlam gyalpo didak chokgi tso
tayé drowa künla pen jé ching
küntou zangpo gyenpé zhoung droub té
ngen song nénam malü tongpar sho

By virtue of the boundless, genuine merit
Gained by fully dedicating excellent conduct,
May all beings engulfed in the great river of suffering
Attain Buddha Amitābha's most excellent domain.

May these sovereign aspiration prayers
Bring about that which is most excellent and sublime,
And may they benefit all beings, infinite in number.
May this scripture adorned by Samantabhadra be accomplished,
And may the entire space of the unfortunate realms become
empty.

འཕགས་པ་བཟང་པོ་སྤྱོད་པའི་སྨོན་ལམ་གྱི་རྒྱལ་པོ་རྫོགས་སོ།

This concludes the Noble King of Aspiration Prayers of Excellent Conduct.

རྒྱ་གར་གྱི་མཁན་པོ་རྫི་ན་མི་ཏྲ་དང་། སུ་རེནྡྲ་པོ་དྷི་དང་།
ཞུ་ཆེན་གྱི་ལོ་ཙྪ་བ་བནྡེ་ཡེ་ཤེས་སྡེ་ལ་སོགས་པས་བསྒྱུར་ཅིང་ཞུས་ཏེ་གཏན་ལ་ཕབ་
པར་ཐབ་པའོ།

This text was finalized by the Indian scholars Dzinamitra and Surendrabodhi and the great editor Lotsawa Bendé Yéshé Dé, among others, who translated and checked it.

—Translator's Note—

Concerning the very last verse, it seems it was added by the original translators and is not found in the Sanskrit original. There are two accepted versions. In many texts—Drakpa Gyaltsen's commentary, for example— the third line reads as above. The one below is found in Tāranātha's commentary on the practice and in some other texts:

།ཀུན་ཏུ་བཟང་པོ་བརྒྱན་པའི་ཞིང་ལྷུང་གྲུབ་སྟེ

küntou zangpo gyenpé zhing droub té

May the pure realms adorned by Samantabhadra be attained,

And may the entire space of the unfortunate realms become empty.

Also, concerning the eighteenth verse, where our wish is to develop boundless communication skills, when Künzig Shamar Rinpoche describes the classes of beings called *yakṣa* and *kimbhāṇḍa* in Sanskrit, they closely resemble the human-like beings in world mythology called djinns, or genies, and trolls. Nāgas are underground or water beings, often depicted as having a half-human, half-snake form.

Translated under the guidance of Künzig Shamar Rinpoche by Pamela Gayle White. Transliteration by Pamela Gayle White.

My sincere apologies for all mistakes. Through the luminous blessing of the masters, may the light of wisdom outshine the translator's murky confusion in all future endeavors.

Publishing finished
in January 2022 by Pulsio
Publisher Number: 4017
Legal Deposit: January 2022
Printed in Bulgaria